MW01490084

Clued In Edinburgh

The Concise and Opinionated Guide to the City

Dean Dalton + Andie Easton

2025 Edition

Includes original images by ©Alan Duke
Contributed image by ©Kanel Bullar

Logo and cover created by Scooter Reyes

designedbyscooter@gmail.com

The world is a big place unless you know where to look.

The Clued In Travel Team

Edinburgh, Scotland

Ah, Edinburgh, how stunning you are! And how mysterious. You're a city with two personalities, and two different sections of town to reflect them. Your medieval Old Town and Georgian-styled New Town could not be more different, and yet somehow strike a balance between the dark and the light of your long history.

The past is evident everywhere here; stone buildings from the 13th century still line the streets and alleyways of the medieval area… never mind that there's a Starbucks tucked inside some of them. This is what Edinburgh is and has been for awhile now: a place that has embraced the new without giving up the very foundations of its historic structure. Visitors will find this is especially true along the bustling "Royal Mile," as it is now called. Formerly the city's High Street, it runs from Edinburgh Castle straight over to the King's Palace of Holyroodhouse.

Edinburgh is an incredibly friendly place and its local folk are ready to engage in conversation anywhere, anytime. Travelers won't take long to realize that even a quick chat with a Scot can easily turn into an in-depth conversation about soccer, politics, or local sights that they heartily recommend. These are a people who love life, who want to share it, and who are never in a hurry to pass up the chance to make a new friend.

This is an affordable city for dining and readily offers up everything from fast food to pub food to well-priced haute cuisine. The food scene here continues to become more and more international, and our suggestions in the upcoming chapter on *Feasting* will reflect this. Even the locals here probably don't eat haggis and blood sausage *all* the time. If you choose only traditional Scottish cuisine for every meal you'll be missing out. Edinburgh is a proud but welcoming place to the rest of the world and that is precisely what is reflected in its modern cuisine.

Visitors to the Scottish capital should note that it's a wee bit too large and too hilly to be completely walkable, though it can be done if you have a good amount of time. City buses, taxi cabs, a modern tramway, and Uber cars are all ready to assist you. Transportation services are relatively inexpensive here and help speed you to wherever you're going. The top sights are either right in the center of town or only a fifteen-minute ride away. From the ancient fortress on the hill to the sheep pastures that reach down to the harbor known as the Firth of Forth, Edinburgh simply could not be more charming to today's explorer. It's well-cared for too, and clean to a fault when compared to centuries ago when a holler of *gardyloo!* meant that the contents of a chamber pot were about to be tossed out a window.

With its famous International Festival, real haunted pubs, royal palace, kitschy ghost tours, and an abundance of free national galleries, Edinburgh definitely offers something for everyone. It boasts truly exquisite art, nearby castles to survey, steep hiking trails, quaint village streams, designer fashion stores, and plaid scarf shops galore. It's a place where the semi-annual pagan bonfire ceremonies are just as important as its quaint Christmas markets. And for those willing to take a bus or taxi to the next village, a visit to the mystifying Rosslyn Chapel should certainly be in order.

Choose a neighborhood from this guide that appeals to you, either by its quirky personality or by its proximity to the particular sights you plan on exploring, and then reserve your accommodations early. Hotel prices are quite fair here especially when booked in advance.

Can a visitor skip the main sights altogether and still enjoy themselves? Absolutely. As one of the most haunted cities in the United Kingdom, let's just say there's never a dull moment, especially on our exclusive haunted pubs crawl. And there are enough street entertainers, bars, bakeries, markets, concerts, soccer matches, and festivals to keep even the biggest history-hater happy. These people can have a terrific time in Edinburgh, but they will never truly understand her.

As for our *Clued In Edinburgh*, let's just say this complicated city truly needs an opinionated guide book. Without candid suggestions, how can a visitor know which sights to wait in line for and which to skip entirely? There are several places that are definite "tourist attractions" and so we've either left those out entirely or put them in our more cautionary chapter. That's why this guide is perfect for the traveler on the move who does not have a month to spend here. Our main chapters are literally titled *Not to be missed*, *Try to fit it in*, and *Skip it unless it's your thing* –so that you can hit the ground running. Have a wee dram of Scotch whisky and then go find your inner *Outlander*, suited to your own interests, for this is a city that holds a different experience for each person. And as we clue you in, we hope you'll find some wisdom in our pages.

-Dean and Andie, and the entire *Clued In* team.

Clued In Edinburgh
The Concise and Opinionated Guide to the City

An Edinburgh street on a rainy day

©Alán Duke

Getting a Clue

Hi there. You're about to explore the most concise city guide you've ever come across. One may ask, "Can a guide book have too much information?" Yes it can. And it can be a frustrating thing to sift through pages and pages of a city's history, analysis of the sewage system, cisterns, and how a building's bricks were laid when all you want to do is know a particular sight is worth your time or not. You won't have that problem here. Our guide is as easy to use as it is to follow, and we'll start with a few basic tips so that you can start investigating everything this incredible city has to offer. You'll find Edinburgh's best sights arranged in the order we thought would be the most interesting to you. This book can help you decide what to do based on the amount of time you have. After the sights, you'll find our heartfelt recommendations for dining, breakfast spots, and pastries. After that are a few hotels we know you'll love, followed by some final notes on the city's free sights, annual events, its major museums, transportation, tips, telephone calling, money issues, and basic safety.

Each entry will provide you with an *at-a-glance* layout of the most necessary details such as the days they are closed, their website address, and interesting highlights that we think you should know. The restaurants even have a rating on the ambience and noise level so you can choose precisely the right vibe you're in the mood for.

As you read on, you'll notice short bullet points labeled *Pro Tip*, *Cultural Tidbit*, *Mealtime Clue*, etc., along with an occasional personal message from us to help give you insight. Don't skip over these points; they're rich with information that will set you apart from other travelers. Here are some good clues to start with...

For specific updates to this edition and more things to see and do here, check out the Edinburgh page of our website, **www.cluedintravelbooks.com**

When to go. The changeable weather of Scotland means you never know what's going to happen but the warmer months (from April to September) are definitely the best for getting the most enjoyment out of a visit here. April boasts the lowest rainfall, but just barely. The largest crowds will descend in August for the annual International Festival but this is also the time when the city is the most fun. Alternatively, the colder off-season means you can visit more sights and enjoy the added benefit of lower hotel and apartment rates (and airfares that are not exorbitant.) While not a highly religious place, Edinburgh celebrates the Christmas season and New Year's with great gusto. Winter can get quite cold so make sure you bring a heavy coat. Edinburgh is so far north that it should be noted the average high temperature in summer is only around 67 degrees Fahrenheit.

The long and short of it: Edinburgh's daylight hours vary greatly from summer to winter with *very* short days in December and very long ones in June and July. For example, late June has sunrise at 4:30am and sunset at 10pm!

Location, location, location.   We believe that the location of your accommodation is paramount. Better to stay in a more humble place near the city center than to stay at a fancy hotel that's three miles out of town. Unless you're in the thick of it, you haven't really experienced it. We prefer the Canongate area for our accommodations but as long as you're in Edinburgh proper and not in the suburbs you'll have a fine time. (See our descriptions of the various neighborhoods, coming up shortly.)

About US passports...   If you need one, it will take awhile so apply for one immediately.   If you already have one, make certain the expiration date will be *more* than four months from the last day of your planned visit. The United Kingdom has strict rules.

An ETA (Electronic Travel Authorization) is now required for Americans and Canadians to enter the United Kingdom. Apply online for entry and pay the fee of £16 (good for two years) at least one week in advance of your travels –and be approved- or you will not be allowed to board your international flight. This ETA *visa-waiver* (as it is called) is required in addition to a current, valid passport. Babies and children are <u>not</u>

exempt from this application process and fee! Visit the official link to apply or learn more:

https://etauk.co.uk

The Historic Scotland "Explorer Pass" is a card that grants entry and discounts on sights and castles across Scotland for either five or fourteen consecutive days. It's a decent value if you plan on visiting the places listed on their plan, especially Edinburgh Castle *and* Stirling Castle (two of our favorites) and allows you to skip the line at both. Having said that, if your plan is to stay put in Edinburgh proper then skip buying it because almost all of Edinburgh's museums and galleries are free. If you're curious check their website:

**www.historicenvironment.scot/visit-a-place/
explorer-passes**

Is it safe to stay near the central train station? You betcha. Edinburgh is unique in that its central rail station, Waverley, is smack dab in the middle of the city and actually very close to several of the most exclusive five-star hotels. This is one train station neighborhood you won't feel seedy about.

A late meal? Not in this town. Okay, maybe at the height of summer but certainly not during the rest of the year. Places close up by 9pm so plan accordingly, especially if you'll be attending an evening show or concert. Plan on eating before the show or you'll be forced to eat fast food. Even the pubs stop serving food by 10pm unless it's the height of the tourist season. The one exception might be the *Grand Café* inside the Scotsman Hotel on North Bridge. Call ahead to be sure at 0-131-622-2999.

Tourist tax: In Edinburgh, hotels and short-term rentals sometimes charge a small daily room tax of around just £3 per room, per day, but a 5% tax will be implemented much later, in July of 2026.

Fahgettaboutit. These days you can forget about bringing large backpacks, oversized bags, and especially luggage of any kind into Scotland's museums, palaces, galleries, and theatres. Most websites now list the maximum measurements of items allowed inside any particular venue.

Accessibility for visitors with limited mobility is surprisingly easy in Edinburgh. Look for our *Stair Scare* warnings throughout this book, including general accessibility mentions for restaurants, so that we can guide you effortlessly from place to place. Some of the city's museums are free for those persons, as well as one companion.

Voltage: Unlike the United States, Scotland has 220 electrical voltage as well as a unique socket and plug style. **Your US plug will not fit into Scotland's sockets.** Yes, that means even the charging cable for your smart phone. Since most electronic items are dual voltage, your main worry will be these sockets. For a few dollars online, you can buy a *US to UK plug adapter* that will enable your US plug to fit into the local wall sockets.

Map it. The maps on your smart phone are more accurate and detailed than any we could hope to include here. Use them. And if you don't want to be bothered finding a connection as you walk around, just take screenshots beforehand of the neighborhoods you intend to explore and view them as an expandable photo whenever you want, and with no connection needed.

In 2025, you need to plan your trip in advance on the internet. The more you do beforehand the smoother and more successful your visit will be. This includes reservations for your accommodations, sight bookings (almost all offer contactless tickets and reservations,) your train travel, tours, and even your nightly meals. Without reservations, you won't get into the most delicious restaurants and the best sights may already be booked up.

These days, this can all be accomplished weeks in advance. *Clued In Edinburgh* gives you all the official websites you'll need in order to plan an unforgettable stay in this extraordinary city. Once your plans are in place, make screenshots of all your important travel info; these can be a real lifesaver especially when that foreign satellite connection isn't cooperating.

The nightlife here is yours to discover. Edinburgh offers a large range of entertainment at night including musical concerts, folk ensembles, live theatre and sweaty nightclubs. You can see the short list of our personal favorites in Part 10, or ask your hotel concierge for current recommendations.

Pharmacies are fairly easy to find. Take note of them as you walk around in case you feel unwell and need to purchase a cure. They all carry the latest products, many of which are homeopathic. Unlike their European counterparts, they are not always marked with any special symbol or signage.

Christmastime: Most of the sights and museums here are closed from December 24 through Dec 26. Most restaurants are shut tight on Christmas Day. If you plan on coming here during this festive time, you may want to add a few more days onto your stay.

Regarding an arrival at Edinburgh's EDI airport: Do not accept the car services of a private citizen, no matter how professional or persuasive they may seem. Official, metered taxi drivers do not leave their vehicles to drum up business at the terminal.

Proceed to the Taxi Rank (queue) outside and look for the cars with taxi roof lights that are waiting their turn. They come in *many colors and shapes* so the looking for the roof light on top is essential.

For American citizens reentering the USA after their travels: We highly recommend using the completely free MPC app (Mobile Passport Control) to speed you through customs upon arrival. Busy airports like JFK can have a two hour wait if you don't use the MPC.

*The city's Old Town still has an abundant
share of medieval buildings*

©Alán Duke

Edinburgh's Neighborhoods

Old Town: The medieval area that is the very heart of Edinburgh. It features Castle Rock and the Royal Mile and includes the smaller neighborhoods of *Canongate, Castlehill, Grassmarket,* and *Cowgate.*

New Town: This is a perfect and proper example of planned neoclassical streets that circle and crescent in the typical Georgian style. It's located right across from the Old Town, separated by the Princes Street Gardens and is the northern heart of the city. Smaller areas within it include *Haymarket, Canonmills,* and *Princes Street.*

Holyrood & Southside: Encompassing Holyrood Park and Arthur's Seat, this neighborhood extends down to include the southern area of the city center including the University of Edinburgh.

Stockbridge: Located just northwest of Edinburgh Castle, this area boasts the beautiful *Dean Village* and is chock full of pubs, bakeries, restaurants and shops. It's basically the western edge of the New Town.

Calton & Broughton: Featuring Calton Hill, the city's monuments, and the royal terraces, this area extends to Broughton Street and is the center of gay life in Edinburgh.

West End: Edinburgh's theater district and conference center is located in the area west of Edinburgh Castle. Smaller areas within it include *Shandwick Place* and *Tollcross.*

Marchmont: This is a suburb south of the city center that borders on The Meadows. It is home to the more affordable hotels and guesthouses.

Leith: Several kilometers north of the city proper, this area encompasses Edinburgh's main harbor, the Firth of Forth. It's pronounced "*Leeth*."

Newhaven: Newhaven is a fishing village just west of Leith and was founded in the 1400s.

Before You Leave Home

[A Basic Checklist]

Make sure that your passports are not within four months of expiring during your trip. A few European countries allow three months, but don't risk it.

Go online to apply for the new ETA approval and pay your fee to enter the UK. The official website is already live: **https://etauk.co.uk**

Take a photo with your smart device (or make a copy to take with you) of your passport's main info page.

Make sure your airplane seats are confirmed beforehand if you want to actually sit with your children or travel partners.

Get £50 *(from a US bank)* before you travel, just to have some on you. Your best exchange rate will come from a Bank ATM here in the UK.

Call your debit and credit card companies before you travel because it never hurts.

Go online to print out a suggested packing list. You won't believe all the things you were going to forget, like those plug adaptors!

Prescription medications should always be packed into your carry-on bag. This is because "checked" baggage can go missing, if even for a day or two.

Measure the luggage you plan on checking in. Its height, width, and depth added together will give you the *linear* measurement; most major carriers allow this to be a maximum of 62". It should also weigh less than fifty pounds to avoid an added fee. A bathroom scale usually works.

Pack a few small adhesive bandages just in case. They take up no space, and having something like this in your toiletries bag can save you precious time should they be needed. Never, ever bring new walking shoes on a trip; break them in well in advance.

Some airports still forbid full sizes of liquid toiletries in your carry-on. Pack travel-sized minis of 100 ml. (3.4 oz.) or less of sunscreens, lotions, perfumes, toothpaste and mouthwash. If you purchase something liquid here to take home, it will have to go inside your checked luggage for the flight home. Buying whisky? Have it shipped!

PART 1
[Not to be Missed]

*His Majesty's home in Edinburgh has a murderous history,
and is our #1 sight*

©Alán Duke

Palace of Holyroodhouse
[Visit King Charles III's Edinburgh home]

You might be surprised to learn that visitors can actually enter one of the active residences of the Royal Family. When the royals are not there, self-tours are offered and give the visitor great access to the property. Not only is it fun to see how the other half lives, its five-hundred-year-old, murderous history means a fascinating visit is in store.

The name *Holyrood* means Holy cross and has been associated with this exact spot since the construction of the Holyrood Abbey whose ruins are still on the property. The palace was built later and was inhabited by James IV and Margaret Tudor, James V, Mary Queen of Scots, James VI, Charles I, Charles II, Bonnie Prince Charlie (Prince Charles Edward Stuart,) George IV, Queen Victoria, and of course the entire Windsor Royal Family.

Walk in their footsteps as you explore drawing rooms, grand halls, and the State Apartments. We think you get the idea… this palace is major and should not be missed. Your visit here includes a free "multimedia" audio-video device that's interactive and the perfect thing for the more curious in your party. The self-guided tour of the interior takes about one hour.

Palace details:

www.rct.uk/visit/palace-of-holyroodhouse

Royal Trust homepage:

www.rct.uk

Entry with a discount can be booked ahead on their website. *The time is flexible for the entire day of your choosing.*

Located in Holyrood Park, Canongate
-in the Old Town, at the eastern end of Canongate Edinburgh

Intl. calling: (001) 44-303-123-7306
Local mobile calling: 0-303-123-7306

Closed on Tuesdays and Wednesdays, except in summer
Closed on Christmas Day
Other closures may occur suddenly so check their online calendar for your dates

Dean says,

"The oldest part of the palace is where King James VI personally confronted midwife, healer, and accused witch, Agnes Sampson before she was judicially tried and found guilty. This was an infamous case that had a hand in spreading witchcraft accusations to all the way to Massachusetts."

Cultural Tidbit:

The church was founded by King David I in 1128 after he experienced a vision on this spot. He saw a stag with a holy cross (or *rood*) shining in its antlers.

Treat Time:

There's a visitor's café on the grounds near the ticketing office. It offers a fairly good variety of items especially if you just want something quick and easy.

Historical Highlight:

When King James IV of Scotland married Lady Margaret Tudor, the royal families of England and Scotland were linked for the first time in history. Prior to this match, they had been bitter enemies. The reason for the marriage was to bring lasting peace to both countries. Their wedding was held right here in 1503, at Holyrood Abbey.

Explore Score:

"David Rizzio, personal assistant and confident to Mary Queen of Scots, was murdered by the queen's husband in a room adjacent to her bedroom. You may be able to find the bloodstains on the floor near the window. Look for the David Rizzio plaque just above it."

Some Stair Scare:

There are several staircases to traverse over the hour-long visit, as well as a wee elevator for those who need it. Because of this, those with limited mobility are allowed a concessionary price and a free companion ticket.

Seen from nearly every neighborhood,
Edinburgh Castle literally beckons visitors

©Alán Duke

Edinburgh Castle and the Royal Mile
[The historic fortress on Castle Rock]

There are just some places that must be visited, especially if they rise to the level of "venerable icon of the city." Edinburgh Castle, built in the 12th century, is one of those places. It rises out of an extinct volcano as if daring you to go up there. And how can you not? Its history is the same as the history of Edinburgh itself.

If you've never been in a castle before –a real castle– then you're in for a treat. Equal parts fortress, royal digs, and military barracks, there's a lot going on here. During your two-hour visit, you get to wander through many different buildings at your own pace and take in things like the modest crown jewels of Scotland, the grand banqueting hall, the prisons, and the National War Museum. The views over the city are breathtaking and on a clear day you can see all the way to the harbor at the Firth of Forth. If you happen to be up there around 1pm, you may even witness the ceremony of the city's famous one-o'clock gun (think modern cannon) being fired off. (Note that it is never fired on Sundays.)

This castle fortress is the most popular sight to visit in all of Scotland so make sure to read through our tips, coming up in the next pages. Timed entrance tickets can be conveniently purchased right on their website.

After your visit to the castle, stroll right out onto the Royal Mile. This lively avenue was and still is the main spine of the Old Town and offers plenty of pubs, shops, restaurants, and extraordinary people-watching. You will probably run into some bagpipe musicians and street performers as well.

www.edinburghcastle.scot

Book their timed-entry tickets ahead online to avoid serious disappointment
Tickets can be purchased in person but are usually sold out on the same day.

Located on Castle Rock
-in the Old Town, at the western end of the Royal Mile
Edinburgh

Intl. calling: (011) 44-131-225-9846
Local mobile calling: 0-131-225-9846

Open daily throughout most of the year
Closed on Christmas Day and December 26

Pro Tip:

Edinburgh Castle is a complex of separate buildings that were added to over time. We like the royal apartments and prisons the most, and St. Margaret's Chapel is definitely worth a look.

Panic Clue:

If you are late for your paid entry time you will be allowed in on the same day; the new time of your entry will be determined by the number of visitors there.

Winter Clue:

The castle gets lit from mid-November to early January. Special effects called the *Castle of Light* turn nighttime visits into something close to a magical enchantment inside and out! If you are in Edinburgh during the holidays, consider a night visit.

Historic Highlight:

Because of Castle Rock itself, it was never easy to wage war upon this fortress. Enemies would instead lay siege on it, and Edinburgh Castle was besieged no less than twenty-three times.

Castle Clue:

Find Laich Hall, also known as The King's dining room. In there you'll see a wee antechamber where Mary Queen of Scots gave birth to James VI in 1566.

Pic Click:

Between the beautiful castle interiors, exteriors, and incredible views of the city around it, you won't know what to take a picture of first!

Andie says,

"I think the re-creations of the former military barracks and prisons are really well done. Check out the layers of hammocks that would have been used by the men held there."

Dean says,

"The giant, historic cannon known as Mons Meg is on display in the yard near St. St. Margaret's Chapel. Built in 1449, it's still one of the largest cannons in the world and in its heyday could blast a huge four-hundred-pound artillery shell two miles."

Mealtime Clue:

After your visit, head down the long stairway that's just out front of the castle on your right-hand side. This leads down to Grassmarket Square and nearby Victoria Street where you'll find a variety of pubs and eateries to choose from. We love the mouthwatering pulled pork sandwiches at Oink on Victoria Street. (Details in the chapter titled *Treats*.)

Some Stair Scare:

About half of the buildings in the castle's complex are easy for visitors with limited mobility. Unfortunately, the royal apartments cannot be as easily accessed.

The Royals loved this boat for decades;
now it's yours to explore

©Alán Duke

Royal Yacht Britannia
[QEII's decommissioned ship hosts visitors]

The harbor in the neighborhood of Leith is now the permanent home of Queen Elizabeth II's ship, the Royal Yacht Britannia and you can go aboard! We adore sights like this where you can see things you never would have if it was still in operation. Walk the same rooms and corridors as the captain and crew, Princess Diana, Winston Churchill, Nelson Mandela, and Frank Sinatra. See the Queen's private stateroom, still furnished just as she left it. Amazing.

The HMY Britannia was used regularly by the royal family from 1953 to 1997 and has been all over the world. The self tour takes you to all five decks, from the bridge to the laundry and everywhere in between, and the fascinating audio accompaniment by way of an excellent handset brings it all to life. The suburb of Leith can be reached by Uber, taxi, or local buses #11 or #22.

www.royalyachtbritannia.co.uk

Book tickets ahead online to skip the ticket queue and avoid serious disappointment.
If you should miss your reserved time slot, you can still enter anytime on the same day. The staff will happily accommodate you.

Located at the Ocean Terminal in Leith
- a suburb of Edinburgh
The ramp to board the yacht is actually accessed from inside the Ocean Terminal Shopping Mall. Once inside, take the elevator to the 2nd floor.

Intl. calling: (011) 44-131-555-8800
Local mobile calling: 0-131-555-8800

Open daily
Closed Christmas Day and New Year's Day

Pro Tip:

You can book a private tour of Britannia with an expert guide who knows absolutely everything. You'll get to board at the entrance previously reserved for the royal family, and will be treated to a glass of champagne.

If you decide to go public instead of private, you're still invited to enjoy the delicious menu offered at the Royal Deck Tea Room. They serve cocktails and tea and give visitors a unique on-board experience.

A visit on board the RYB (without stopping to eat or drink) runs about ninety minutes.

Andie says,

"In the state room used by Princess Diana, look in the far mirror to see exact copies of her clothes hanging in the closet."

Dean says,

"The yacht could comfortably accommodate two-hundred and fifty guests at one time!"

No Stair Scare:

The RYB is fully accessible for those with limited mobility. It has royal elevators onboard.

The Queen could certainly entertain
on a large scale on this yacht

©*Alán Duke*

Transport Clue:

If you decide to take the local bus to Leith, make sure you have some coins for the fare which is around £2 per person each way. (Some Edinburgh buses are accepting ApplePay but you never know which ones.) The *Ocean Terminal Shopping Centre & Britannia* is the final stop.

Mealtime Clue:

Book ahead for a fancy lunch at the Michelin-starred *Kitchin*. (Details in our chapter titled *Feasting*.)

The mysterious Rosslyn Chapel can be reached by Edinburgh's city buses

©Alán Duke

Rosslyn Chapel
[The mysterious *DaVinci Code* chapel]

Perhaps you didn't realize that the enigmatic Rosslyn Chapel of symbols and lost meanings is located just twenty minutes from Edinburgh. This gem is easy to get to and is much more fascinating than the *DaVinci Code* movie portrays. Take in the free lecture by a local expert and then explore its nooks and crannies. Every inch is carved with flowers, stars, or other unusual designs including corn, camels, a bagpipes-playing angel, and the mysterious pagan "green men."

Does the chapel have a connection to the infamous Knights Templar, or to the Holy Grail itself? No one really knows but we think this amazing place is definitely worth your time.

When you're down in the crypt, notice the coloration on the carvings; these have been naturally preserved from the darkness but experts believe that the entire chapel was once painted in this colorful way. For important transport info, see our advice below.

www.rosslynchapel.com

Booking tickets ahead online for your preferred time is highly recommended.

Located at the Chapel Loan
In nearby Roslin, Midlothian County

Intl. calling: (011) 44-131-440-2159
Local mobile calling: 0-131-440-2159

Open daily
Closed on Christmas Eve, Christmas Day, New Year's Eve, and New Year's Day

Pro Tip:

Time-slots for your entry booking are ninety-minutes long. You can enter anytime during this period, but must leave when it ends.

Dean says,

"The chapel is located in the town of Roslin, spelled in the modern way. The chapel itself has retained the old spelling of *Rosslyn*."

Historical Highlight:

The chapel dates from the Middle Ages, around 1446, and is still owned by the family who built it. It took forty years to build and remains a place of worship to this day.

Transport Clues:

Take a car service or taxi cab for the thirty-minute drive out to Roslin, or save a heap by catching the **Penicuik Deanburn #37 bus** from one of the stops along Princes Street, or at North Bridge or South Bridge. The one-way, per person fare is around £2 and it will drop you at the Roslin Hotel stop which is near the entrance of the chapel property. Easy!

If you want to take a taxi back into Edinburgh after your visit, you'll need to have the chapel's staff call one for you. Another option is to go inside the nearby Roslin Hotel and ask them to call. Or just take the bus back.

Andie says,

"You might see the chapel's resident cat, William, who wandered in as a kitten and simply never left."

Some Stair Scare:

Most sections of Rosslyn Chapel are accessible to those with limited mobility except, for example, the wee crypt below the altar.

Explore Score:

If you like hiking and nature, take the easy thirty-minute walk from the chapel to see what's left of the ruined Rosslyn *Castle*. Use Google map "directions" on your smart phone so that you don't head the wrong way through the dense trees.

Cultural Tidbit:

All proceeds go directly to support the Rosslyn Chapel Trust and help to maintain this historic church.

Mealtime Clue:

The visitors' center has a wee café with homemade soups and light fare. For something heartier, drive or take the local bus a few stops to *The Radhuni*, a delicious, award-winning Indian restaurant right there in Roslin. Local mobile calling:
0-131-440-3566

The incredible, full-access visit of Craigmillar Castle
will take you to another century

©Alán Duke

Craigmillar Castle
[A medieval castle, a magical experience]

We hesitate to call this castle "ruined" because it is rather intact, save for its interiors. In fact, Craigmillar is one of the best well-preserved medieval castles in all of Scotland and happens to be right in Edinburgh. As a visitor, you're usually given full reign to explore *all of it* at your own pace without anything standing between you and the raw history of the place. May Queen of Scots actually stayed here for several weeks.

Trust us; this place is really something to see. And the views over Edinburgh from its battlements are remarkable. Considering its cheapy-cheap admission price, this may be the best deal in Scotland.

www.historicenvironment.scot/visit-a-place/places/craigmillar-castle

Book tickets ahead online to skip the queue and avoid disappointment.
Tickets can be purchased in person if available.

Located on Craigmillar Castle Road
An eleven-minute drive from the city center
Edinburgh

Intl. calling: (011) 44-131-661-4445
Local mobile calling: 0-131-661-4445

Open daily
The grounds around the castle are always free to visit

Closed on Christmas Day and December 26, as well as January 1 & 2

Pro Tip:

This important castle ruin is located just two and a half miles from the city center and is easily accessed by Uber or taxi.

Andie says,

"I love Craigmillar Castle. It's my favorite sight to visit in all of Edinburgh."

Dean says,

"Since inclement weather can often impact the castle's opening times, take a moment to check their website before heading over because they post any sudden closures there, on the right-hand side of the page."

Stair Scare:

This castle is bare bones. Wear sensible shoes or sneakers when visiting here and be sure to watch your step as you discover its secrets. Its interior is not accessible to those with limited mobility.

Historical Highlight:

This castle has a vast history. It was visited and used by several Scottish kings over the centuries for everything from escaping the plague, to secret meetings, or just to enjoy the fine hunting that the area offered. The brother of King James III was held in the wee prison here after being accused of practicing witchcraft against the sovereign.

Cultural Tidbits:

Mary Queen of Scots met with her advisors at Craigmillar Castle to solve the problem of her treasonous husband, Lord Darnley who was later found murdered. This castle has been used in several movies, and is the filming location of the fictional Ardmuir Prison in the series *Outlander*.

Queue Clue:

There's rarely a crowd here because the tourists visiting Edinburgh don't stray this far from the city center. On a weekday in the off-season, you may well have the place to yourself.

*The Scottish National Gallery boasts masterpieces
from around the world*

©Alán Duke

Scottish National Gallery Art Complex
[A splendid collection of paintings by the masters]

Are you in the mood to gaze upon some artistic masterpieces? If so, the neoclassical complex of the Scottish National Gallery/ Royal Scottish Academy is waiting for you. The National Gallery houses the permanent collections of expertly curated paintings. It offers visitors the chance to get up close and personal with works from daVinci, Raphael, Botticelli, Titian, Rembrandt, Vermeer, Turner, Monet, Van Gogh, and Gauguin, as well as some incredible paintings by Scottish artists. Don't miss the second level; you'll find a staircase in the back that will take you there.

At once both intimate and elegant, this wee museum has achieved what other more famous ones have not: vast splendor in a neat and comfortable space. For truly great art that can be enjoyed in a short amount of time, this place packs a wallop.

Note: Next door you'll find the Royal Scottish Academy housing the *temporary* exhibits. Try to pop into both museums because you never know what might be on loan at the Academy. After all, they're free!

www.nationalgalleries.org/visit/scottish-national-gallery

Free to enter
No pre-booking needed

Located on The Mound
-in the city center, off Princes Street, near Hanover Street
Edinburgh

Intl. calling: (011) 44-131-624-6200
Local mobile calling: 0-131-624-6200

Open daily
Closed on some major holidays

Historical Highlight:

These gorgeous neoclassical buildings were built in 1859.

Andie says,

"Local Scots refer to the Scottish National Gallery & Royal Scottish Academy as simply *the galleries.*"

Dean says,

"There's a special Gallery Bus that carries visitors to all of the city's 'national' gallery museums. It goes from the Portrait Gallery (which is near the classical art galleries) and then heads for both the Modern 1 and Modern 2 buildings that are more than a mile away. It only comes around once an hour though so it's not ideal. The fee of £1 is evidently optional."

Queue Clue:

Because the galleries are free, there's never a wait to enter. Just walk right in the front door.

Treat Time:

There's a new Scottish Café & Restaurant on the lower level of the National Gallery. It specializes in sustainable regional foods.

Some Stair Scare:

Visitors must climb a stairway to reach the floor that houses paintings by the Impressionist artists (when it reopens.) Only sections on the main level are accessible to those with limited mobility. This will change in the future after some ongoing renovations.

Mealtime Clue:

Masterpieces can make you hungry but luckily, you're only a five-minute walk from a delicious lunch at Makars Mash. Exit the Mound heading south and then walk up North Bank Street. (Details in our chapter titled *Feasting*)

Another wee dram of whisky please...

Uhh, okay… the closest pub is Milnes of Rose Street, just a block up Hanover Street. Head north from the galleries and make a right onto Rose (right at the start of the New Town.)

Watch out for gnomes as you explore
Edinburgh's secret Dean Village

©Alán Duke

Dean Village & the Water of Leith
[A village and river walk, right in the city center]

Some days you just want to leave the sights behind and commune with the nature of a place. This is not only possible right in the city center of Edinburgh, it's positively unreal. Dean Village, as it is called, is a little piece of Scottish heaven that runs along both sides of the Water of Leith (Edinburgh's river.) Take a morning stroll through its centuries-old architecture, winding pathways, and moss-laden trees. Find the cascade and explore a neoclassical wellhead. If you were ever going to see a gnome or faerie in Scotland, this is where they would be. Quaint doesn't even begin to describe it.

Free public area/ Always open

Located along the Dean Path in the New Town
-you'll find this village right between the two main sections of the city

- Enter from Queensferry Road (Old Town)

- Enter from Saunders Street (New Town)

Andie says,

"This adorable area is easy to find if you walk west on Princes Street and then head north on busy Queensferry Road for a few blocks. Turn when you see the sign marking the *Dean Path* and head to the *Water of Leith Walkway*. From there you can take the winding stroll across a wee bridge and then on up towards the New Town area. Takes about twenty minutes if you don't stop for selfies!"

Dean says,

"The classical, Grecian-looking temple along the path is one of several elaborate 19th century wells."

Historical Highlight:

The village was originally an area of water mills and their owners. You can still spot carved plaques of stone that advertise pies or bread. The tall stone bridge you'll see is the impressive Dean Bridge which rises up over one-hundred feet high. It was built in 1831.

Treat Time:

Just east of the village entrance at Queensferry Road there's a Söderberg Bakery. We can't resist their plump Swedish-style sweet rolls. Stop in for a quick pick-me-up before your stroll. (Details in our chapter titled *Breakfast, Lunch & Treats*)

Stair Scare:

This natural area is not accessible to those with limited mobility.

The intriguing lobby of the Scottish National Portrait Gallery

©Alán Duke

Scottish National Portrait Gallery
[Scotland's famous personalities on display]

Following in the British tradition of portrait galleries, Edinburgh has curated a remarkable one. You'll see very famous Scotsmen and the women they loved, as well as several paintings of the would-be savior of the country, Bonnie Prince Charlie. There's a fascinating library section too, with discreet drawers that you can open to see what's kept inside; their wee treasures include a collection of miniature portraits. Make sure to visit the top floor where the best paintings are kept, and make time to enjoy their truly delicious Portrait Café.

www.nationalgalleries.org/visit/scottish-national-portrait-gallery

Free to enter
No pre-booking needed

Located at 1 Queen Street
-in the city center
,Edinburgh

Intl. calling: (011) 44-131-624-6200
Local mobile calling: 0-131-624-6200

Open daily
Closed from Christmas Eve through December 26

Historical Highlight:
The gallery boasts a magnificent full-length portrait of Mary Queen of Scots. It was painted in 1610, well after her beheading.

Explore Score:

In the gallery's breathtaking grand hall, look up at the timeline mural and see if you can spot Robert the Bruce and William Wallace. Hint: they are in medieval garb and are standing next to each other.

Andie says,

"The paintings here have plaques next to them that are very informative. They tell you who the artist was and explain something about the person *in* the painting. Learning something about the life of the subject makes for a very interesting visit."

Mealtime Clue:

Have a delicious lunch right inside the gallery at Café Portrait. They're open when the museum is, closing thirty minutes before the end of the visiting hours. Their fresh, creative offerings, like Brie, Blueberry, & Walnut Quiche, are all made on the premises from scratch. The prices are quite low; book ahead online during high season if you're counting on eating there. Local mobile call: 0-131-558-7031.

No Stair Scare:

This portrait gallery is accommodating to those with limited mobility.

Edinburgh's historic cathedral is called St. Giles'

©*Alán Duke*

St. Giles' Cathedral
[The city's gorgeous High Kirk]

Like most of the grand capitals in the UK and Europe, Edinburgh boasts a splendid cathedral. It's the premier place of worship of the Church of Scotland in this city and while not the official seat of any Bishop (the formal definition of a cathedral) this high church, or *kirk* in Gaelic, was named for St. Giles, a popular hermit in the Middle Ages. He also holds the honor of being the patron saint of Edinburgh itself.

The earliest version of this structure was built in the 14th century and has served as the center of Edinburgh's religious activity for over eight-hundred years. You'll spot its tall, crown-shaped spire before you get even close to it. Go inside and be dazzled.

www.stgilescathedral.org.uk

Free to enter

Located on High Street
-in the Old Town (aka the Royal Mile, just a block from the castle esplanade)
Edinburgh

Intl. calling: (011) 44-131-226-0674
Local mobile calling: 0-131-226-0674

Closed Sundays, except for worship

Pic Click:

The cathedral welcomes the taking of photos and videos (without flash) but asks that you first place money into their donation box first; it can be found just inside the entrance.

Historical Highlight:

After the Scots signed a declaration of independence from England, the English King, Edward II sent an army to Edinburgh with the clear intent of causing as much damage as possible. It was during this raid in 1322 that the cathedral was burned in a massive fire. Much of the city was burned down as well.

Andie says,

"This is a working church so be sure to show respect and speak softly when inside the nave."

Dean says,

"There are many concerts held here, some at midday and some at night. Check their website for upcoming performances."

Hidden Gem:

Rooftop visits of St. Giles' cathedral are offered on weekends. It is a guided tour, and limited to four people at a time for a small fee. Email your request to: info@stgilescathedral.com - or visit their welcome desk.

Some Stair Scare:

This church is accessible via ramps at the main entrance into the building.

Another wee dram of whisky please!

Are you kidding? Well, you've got the beautiful (and famous) Deacon Brodies Tavern just over there, one block up the street.

A visit to the famous Stirling Castle is an easy journey

©Alán Duke

Stirling Castle

[One of Scotland's largest & most important castles]

Half-day excursion

Stirling Castle is a grand 14th century fortress with a significant story to tell. Set in the countryside less than an hour by direct train from Edinburgh's central station, it simply had to be included this chapter. The castle was built on a hill above the village of Stirling which grew from its association with the royal residence. Even so, Stirling maintains its small-town personality to this day.

The doomed queen, Mary Queen of Scots was crowned here at just nine months old after her father, James V had died from a sudden illness. The castle was hers for the rest of her twenty-four-year reign though she did move about to other castles that were under her charge. The place has been inhabited by Scottish Kings before and after her, and has endured at least eight sieges. It's amazing that it still stands. Historic in every regard, and visited by thousands of people every year, this castle thrives because it has never been abandoned or neglected.

Some people say that it has recently been restored to such a high degree that something indefinable has been lost. We have nothing against much-needed restoration of course, but the interiors of the royal lodgings are now somewhat modern in their construction and have added decoration, paint, and faux moldings that are meant to give today's visitor a suggestion of what it all may have once looked like. The expensive endeavor includes re-creations of bedrooms, kitchens, and other decor along with some costumed employees ready to answer your questions. Even the famous Unicorn Tapestries of James V hanging in the Queen's Presence Chamber are re-creations, though done to exacting specifications, because the real ones are now in New York City. (Paris has a different set of Unicorn tapestries, also from the Middle Ages.)

These "improvements" mean that visitors can appreciate how the castle looked during its heyday, and how its interiors looked to its royal residents. Whether you like the renovations or not, you're still visiting a structure where many important Scottish events took place.

The views of the surrounding countryside are gorgeous and you can even walk along the protective walls in a nearly 360-degree arc. From there you'll see the tall tower of the William Wallace Monument in the distance, marking the spot of one of his most famous battles against the English. Those familiar with the film *Braveheart* will have an immense appreciation.

www.stirlingcastle.scot

Book tickets ahead online to skip the queue and avoid disappointment.
Their website offers a discount compared to purchasing tickets at the door.

Located high up the hill, on Castle Esplanade
In the town of Stirling, Scotland

Intl. calling: (011) 44-178-645-0000
Local mobile calling: 0-178-645-0000

Open daily to visitors with reservations
Closed on Christmas Day & December 26

Pro Tip:

Getting to Stirling from Edinburgh is a breeze. There are forty direct trains a day from Waverley Station and run nearly every half hour. The cost is fair at around £20 round trip (though off-peak times can be even cheaper.) It's a thirty-mile journey and takes about fifty minutes. The train's webpage is:

www.thetrainline.com/train-times/Edinburgh-waverley-to-stirling

Dean says,

"The Waverley Station ticketing machines are easy to use and take credit cards. If you would rather pay in cash, head to the middle of the station and enter the official ticketing lounge. On the Waverley departure board, the train you want will be labeled *Dunblane* even though your stop will be *Stirling*. Note that on most of these trains you *must* push a button to open the carriage door to board, and then again to exit. They are not automatic."

Train Clue:

Keep track of your train tickets because you'll need them *three* times in each direction: 1) for the turnstiles that lead to the platforms, 2) on board for the conductor, and 3) to get through the exit turnstiles at your destination. Keep them in a safe place!

Castle Clue:

Both Mary and her father, James V, were crowned at Stirling Castle.

Andie says,

"In Stirling, there's a cute trolley called a 'land train' that shuttles visitors from the area of the rail station right up to the castle esplanade. It runs during the Easter holidays and also in summer. It costs only £1 and children five and under are free. Catch it in front of the *Our Place Café* located on Murray Place. This is the street just up the hill from the Stirling Train Station. It can take a half hour to show up, however so if you don't see it you should consider walking up or taking a taxi; it's not expensive and will get you there much faster."

Treat Time:

The castle has its own eatery called the Unicorn Café which is located in the castle courtyard. It offers sandwiches, snacks, and an assortment of beverages.

Some Stair Scare:

Much of Stirling Castle has been adapted to be accessible to those with limited mobility. There's even a courtesy vehicle that you can call for help if anyone in your party has difficulty with steep inclines and steps. Just call 0-1786-450-000 before your visit (or ask a staff member about it once you arrive) so that you can use the vehicle to get back down the hill.

Pic Click:

Between the beautiful castle and the views of the historic area around it, you won't know what to take a picture of first!

Hidden Gem:

Stirling's beautiful and historic 'Church of the Holy Rude' lies a wee bit southwest of the castle area and can be visited. When Mary Queen of Scots was forced to abdicate in 1567, her infant son James VI was crowned King of Scots at its altar. You can get more information about visiting the church by calling the folks there at 0-178-647-5275

Panic Clue:

If you are late for your paid entry time you will be allowed in on the same day; the new time of your entry will be determined by the number of visitors there.

PART 2
[Try to Fit it in]

Victoria Street & Grassmarket Square
[The street that inspired J.K. Rowling]

It's just not a visit to Edinburgh without a quick stop at picturesque Victoria Street. This colorful sloped-and-curving street near the Greyfriars Kirkyard (graveyard) and Grassmarket Square in the city's Old Town evidently caught the attention of local author J.K. Rowling when she was writing her first *Harry Potter* book. Definitely a Diagon Alley of sorts, Victoria Street is a hodge-podge of cute little shops including one dedicated to magic. Rowling used to do some of her writing at the Elephant House Café which is only a block away, and that graveyard was obviously of great inspiration to her; several of her character's names were borrowed from the tombstones there.

The steep alleyway of the old West Bow Street was refashioned in 1834 into the curved street we see today and renamed to honor the young Queen Victoria. But on the West Bow Street of the seventeenth century, a real wizard resided there... well-known resident, Major Weir was initially regarded as a Godly man who could do no wrong but eventually his evil deeds caught up with him. He was tried for the crimes of necromancy and black magic and even admitted to it. He was executed for witchcraft in 1670 and his house was left empty for a hundred years because locals were afraid to go near it. It was finally destroyed when the street was rebuilt.

At the bottom of the sloping street is Grassmarket Square, the main square of the entire Old Town.

Free public area/ always open

Located east of Edinburgh Castle
-in the Old Town, between George IV Bridge & Grassmarket Square
Edinburgh

Andie says,

"Look up and you'll see the pedestrian-only Victoria Terrace that runs along the tops of the shops. You can access it from George IV Bridge and connect right to Johnston Terrace which is the road that runs along the bottom of Castle Rock."

Dean says,

"Predictably, there's now a Harry Potter themed boutique on Victoria Street. Also look for two of our standouts: I. J. Mellis Cheesemongers and Oink."

Treat Time:

Depending on the time of day and what you're in the mood for, we can heartily recommend either Oink for a delectable pulled pork sandwich right on Victoria Street, or a creamy *gelato* at Mary's Milk Bar in nearby Grassmarket Square. *(Details about Oink are in our chapter titled Breakfast, Lunch, & Treats)*

Mealtime Clue:

For the best food in Grassmarket Square, wait for a table at the delicious and popular Mussel and Steak Bar. (Details in our chapter titled *Feasting*)

Another wee dram of whisky please!

Again? Well, there's the Bow Bar right on Victoria Street, and about seven more pubs in Grassmarket Square. Just keep walking downhill, if you can.

No Stair Scare:

Other than a pot hole or two, this public area can accommodate those with limited mobility.

Performances at the Lyceum are always memorable

©Alán Duke

Royal Lyceum Theatre
[Top notch shows in an antique theatre]

As one of the city's premiere performance spaces, The Lyceum is almost unaltered from its original 1883 Victorian design. It's like an old-fashioned candy box, and boasts just over six-hundred seats. The discerning group of professionals behind the Lyceum today prides itself on producing many original, modern works. When you book tickets for one of their shows, you can have confidence that it be a truly memorable evening. This is the *grand dame* of the Scottish theatre scene. Treat yourself.

https://lyceum.org.uk

You'll find a wide range of prices for seats available on their website.
Now accepting bookings by phone or online.

Located at 30B Grindlay Street
-in the Old Town
Edinburgh

Intl. calling: (011) 44-131-248-4848 (Box Office)
Local mobile calling: 0-131-248-4848

Their telephone ticket service is open Monday through Friday from 10am to 5pm

Andie says,

"This theatre, like so many places in Edinburgh, is very haunted. There's a blue lady who is seen quite often, as well as a shadow figure and an unexplainable ringing sound that can occur."

Dean says,

"This theatre was the first in all of Scotland to have electric lighting installed."

Cultural Tidbit:

The Lyceum is always part of the International Festival which takes place annually in August. (Details in our chapter titled *The Edinburgh International Festival*.)

Historical Highlight:

The Lyceum's opening night in 1883 featured famed Shakespearean actor Henry Irving in *Much Ado About Nothing*.

Treat Time:

There's ice cream for sale at the lobby bar during intermission!

Stair Scare:

The Lyceum offers accessible seating for some performances to those with limited mobility on the main level. Call them with any questions you might have.

Mealtime Clue:

It's not easy to find late night dining in this city so be sure to book an early dinner to enjoy *before* the performance.

*Surround yourself in the history, bottling,
and sheer variety of whisky*

©Alán Duke

The Scotch Whisky Experience
[Become an educated whisky drinker]

When it comes to drinking, the Scots definitely know what's what. That's why there are several distilleries in town that welcome visitors. Two of them are Gin distilleries which strikes us as more English than Scottish so our recommendation is to pay a visit to the Scotch Whisky Experience where you'll learn everything about the local favorite. (Yes, that's really how they spell *whisky* in Scotland.)

Is it a tourist attraction? Well yes, but we still recommend it. Visitors start the interactive tour with a ride in a private barrel, and end inside a room boasting the world's largest whisky collection. In between they learn all about the production, history and different regions of this Scottish treat. It's a modern, full immersion experience and by the end you'll be knowledgeable enough to choose the perfect dram, just like a connoisseur. Even if you don't like the "darker pours" you'll walk away with a new appreciation of them. *Slanjevah!*

www.scotchwhiskyexperience.co.uk

Tickets with timed-entry can be booked ahead online to avoid disappointment.

-Persons under age 18 (or who don't drink alcohol) can have a great time here and are given other choices of beverage at the tasting.

Located on the Royal Mile
-in the Old Town, just before the castle esplanade
Edinburgh

Intl. calling: (011) 44-131-220-0441
Local mobile calling: 0-131-220-0441

Open daily
Closed on Christmas Day

The Basic Silver Tour Includes:

A whisky barrel ride through the production of Scotch whisky, a cask room, introduction to the aromas in whisky, regions of certain whiskies, a dram of Scotch whisky or the local *Irn Bru* to sample, viewing of the world's largest private collection of unopened Scotch whiskies, and a gift of a crystal tasting glass (for adults and seniors.)

Pro Tip:

They offer various experiences to choose from, all more intense than the *Silver*. There are also master classes that you can attend.

Great Clue:

An audio guide is available (in 20 languages) if requested. In addition, there are multi-language speaking employees on staff.

Cultural Tidbit:

The word *whisky* is derived from an old Gaelic word meaning *water of life*. This tells you how serious the Scots are about their favorite spirit.

Andie says,

"I'm not a whisky drinker but I really enjoyed this entire experience."

Pic Click:

It's not everyday you find yourself surrounded by eight-thousand bottles of whisky, including one from 1897… go ahead, take a video!

Dean says,

"Well, I *am* a whisky drinker so it was great that I could choose the *Gold* experience and get a fuller experience with more drams and yet still be on the same tour as Andie who paid for the basic *Silver* experience. The visit takes about fifty minutes."

Stair Scare:

The Scotch Whisky Experience is fully accessible to those with limited mobility.

Mealtime Clue:

Their Amber Restaurant is right on the premises and can be visited by anyone wishing to dine, not just those who took the tour. It regularly stocks some four-hundred and twenty-two different whiskies in case you still need to keep comparing the notes of the different regions.

Tour Edinburgh's largest "close"
which is now completely underground

©Alán Duke

The Real Mary King's Close
[An underground tour
where the poorest once lived]

The many *closes* (alleyways) that run out from either side of old Edinburgh's High Street (now called the Royal Mile) might remind you of ribs sticking out from a long spine. That's actually a good way to think of it, but there's much more to these strange offshoots. They were tiny, crowded streets where the poorest folks from the Middle Ages through the 18th century would shop, work, drink, gather, hang out, and access their barely-livable, no-plumbing hovels that were located there.

The rest of the town was not really socially open to these people, nor was it safe for them to venture out of these *closes*. The wealthier folk lived on High Street or, at the very least, on the upper-most floors of the buildings along the *close* which enjoyed more light and less of the foul stench.

This tourist attraction explores one of the city's largest, the Mary King's Close, which was covered over when the area was needed to the build the offices of the Royal Exchange. Rather than kicking out all the people living on the lower street, it was simply covered over. This plunged the residents there into total darkness with only a single opening at either end of the *close*.

These fully guided, one-hour underground tours are quite thoughtful and explore the past in an intimate way as you progress through actual pathways, residences and workshops that were essentially preserved when they were covered. We believe it is worth your time but take a moment to heed our warning below before you book it.

www.realmarykingsclose.com

Book your tickets weeks ahead online to avoid disappointment

Visitors' entrance located at 2 Warriston's Close,
-in the Old Town, across from St. Giles' Cathedral
Edinburgh

Intl. calling: (011) 44-131-225-9442
Local mobile calling: 0-131-225-9442

Tours held on most days; check their online calendar
Closed on Christmas Day

Wee Warning:

Some of the hovels that visitors are allowed to see are small and have low ceilings. Even though the tour groups are kept to fewer visitors than ever before, some people may experience a bit of claustrophobia. If this should happen, the affected visitor can simply be guided out by a staff member. (A dram of whisky before the tour might be of some use here.)

Pro Tip:

Tours depart every fifteen minutes and can be booked ahead online if there's a particular time that you wish to secure.

Dean says,

"There were usually a few cattle kept inside the close; these animals would just make themselves at home here, right outside the tenements."

Historical Highlight:

Gardyloo! (an anglicized version of *garde à l'eau!* or "watch out for the water!" in French) was hollered every morning and every night to warn those outside that the chamber pots were about to be thrown out a window or doorway.

Andie says,

"Being able to see where the poorest lived gives you a whole different perspective of medieval times in Edinburgh. By the way, the word *close* is pronounced just like in the sentence: *those walls are really close together.* That's probably where it came from!"

Pic Click:

While there's no photography allowed on the tour, the staff does arrange groups for a dramatic photo that will be available for a fee as you exit. There's no obligation to buy it, but it could make for a memorable souvenir. Having said that, you're certainly welcome to tell the tour guide that you don't wish to pose for the photo.

Stair Scare:

This historic underground venue cannot accommodate certain visitors with limited mobility. Check their online accessibility guide for answers to your questions.

The views from atop Calton Hill are unreal

©Alán Duke

Calton Hill
[The city's monuments and a stupendous view]

It sometimes seems like every great photo of Edinburgh is taken from this hill, and that's because so many are! That means you need to climb it and have a look for yourself. Calton Hill is this city's choice when it comes to placing monuments, perhaps because there's little space left within their grid of streets and alleyways.

Calton Hill is the name of both an area *and* an actual hill and together they make up the neighborhood at the east end of Princes Street. While the vicinity boasts quiet residential streets, it's also known for the Edinburgh Playhouse, the Collective contemporary gallery, the city's gay bars, and the cafés and bakeries of busy Broughton Street.

The hill itself, now a UNESCO World Heritage Site, is easy to hike up to and takes less than ten minutes from the Waverley Station in the center of town. It can be accessed from a staircase on Regent Road to the south, from the Royal Terrace to the north, or you can drive up. Once there you'll see a handy path that runs around the edge of the hill. Visit the various monuments at your leisure or pop into the new observatory. (The old observatory was turned into The Collective art gallery which can also be visited.)

The large monument of classical columns is the Scottish National Monument, or merely the *National Monument*, which in 1816 was meant to be a kind of Parthenon to commemorate Napoleon's defeat at Waterloo and all those who died in the Napoleonic Wars. The tall tower is Nelson's Monument, built to honor Admiral Nelson for his victory at Trafalgar;

climb its one-hundred-forty-three spiral steps to the top if you're feeling energetic. The round temple is the Dugald Stewart Monument and honors one of Scotland's most famous philosophers. There are also several smaller monuments you can check out.

Perhaps the best thing about climbing up Calton Hill is the incredible view over the city. Take a moment to appreciate the nearby Salisbury Crags and Arthur's Seat hilltop, formations that were created by an ancient volcano. Time your visit with the sunset to get some truly beautiful photographic shots.

No official website

Free public space

Located in the city center
-in the city center, at the eastern end of Princes Street
Edinburgh

Always open

Historical Highlight:

The hill was once known for its monastery, but after Scotland's reformation it was abandoned and stayed empty for some time. After 1591, it became a quarantine hospital for lepers.

Pic Click:

Taking a truly great photograph of Edinburgh is one of the main reasons for coming up here.

Andie says,

"Calton Hill Road was the main street of an old village that dominated the area. A group of stone houses from 1760 that can be seen at the top of it are all that remain."

Dean says,

"The stairway that we take to reach the top of Calton Hill is located right on Regent Road, near the large government building there. The base of these steps is marked by a rectangle relief of three profiles, a memorial to three 19th century Scottish singers."

Some Stair Scare:

The hill and monuments are not easily accessible to those with limited mobility, but sections of it are possible. Take a taxi as close as you can get to it.

Fireworks Fun:

Calton Hill provides unforgettable viewing of the city's fireworks during both *Hogmanay* (New Year's celebration) and the grand conclusion of the Edinburgh International Festival usually in August. It's also one of the locations used for the bonfires of the Beltane Fire Festival (in the spring) and also the Samhuinn Fire Festival at Halloween.

Royal Botanic Garden
[Lush grounds and spectacular glasshouses]

In the northern section of Edinburgh's beautiful New Town, lucky visitors will find the Royal Botanic Garden. This lavish place of flowers, plants, glass greenhouses, and restaurants is a lovely and peaceful way to spend a morning. The 350-year-old grounds boast 100,000 plants from around the world, cultivated on seventy acres and inside ten glasshouses ranging in climates from tropical to desert.

Their *Chinese Hillside* garden is one of the largest collections of Chinese plants outside of the Far East and actually recreates the natural experience of climbing a hill in southwest China.

If you don't know much about plants, take their guided tour and gain a new understanding of the greener things in our world. We think this is one of the best botanical gardens anywhere.

www.rbge.org.uk/visit/royal-botanic-garden-edinburgh

Free to enter
No pre-booking needed

Located on Arboretum Place
-in the New Town
Edinburgh

Intl. calling: (011) 44-131-248-2909
Local mobile calling: 0-131-248-2909

Open daily
Closed Christmas Day and New Year's Day

Note that some of the glasshouses are closed for restoration this year.

Andie says,

"I love flowers, but I also love animals! That's why I'm going to take one second here to mention that Edinburgh also has a pretty great zoo. It's located a couple of miles west of the city center and has Giant Pandas as well as the only Koalas in the United Kingdom."

Mealtime Clue:

The Garden's own Terrace Café provides lovely dining on the premises, or opt for a brunch of pancakes and crispy bacon at the nearby Bluebird Café. Bluebird's telephone number is 0-44-774-997-1847 and they're open until 3pm on most days.

No Stair Scare:

The gardens are almost completely accessible to those with limited mobility.

Visit the past at nearby Lauriston Castle

©Alán Duke

Lauriston Castle
[A historic home, completely intact]

Mini-excursion

Well, this is as real as it gets. Actually, more of a stately 16th century home than a true castle, Lauriston remains a very special place. Its many well-to-do past residents are steeped in history and all had a hand in decorating its interiors over the centuries. The style you'll see during your visit is Edwardian and is nearly untouched from the day the entire estate was left to the Historic Trust by Mrs. Reid in 1926. Every book, linen, and furnishing is original and belonged to her and her husband. No wonder the place is haunted.

Small-group tours on certain days by locals who know all the details about the place are offered. Visitors must book ahead online. Conversely, the landscaped grounds around the castle are open to the public from morning to night and are free of charge. They feature a Japanese garden and rolling lawns with sweeping views of a sheep meadow and the harbor at Firth of Forth. For those who want a thorough historical experience that's just a quick car or taxi ride from downtown Edinburgh, this is your place.

www.edinburghmuseums.org.uk/venue/lauriston-castle

Pre-booking of their various tours is required
Visit the website above to reserve your dates

Located at 2 Cramond Road South
-in a northern suburb of Edinburgh

Intl. calling: (011) 44-131-336-2060
Local calling: 0-131-336-2060

Note their current seasonal schedule on their website
-sometimes only open on Saturdays and Sundays
Always closed on Mondays and major holidays

Pro Tip:

This fascinating place is in the countryside just four miles from Edinburgh's city center and is easily reached by Uber or taxi. You *must* book ahead because their tours almost always sell out.

Great Clue:

A very scenic trip from Edinburgh to Lauriston Castle can be made by bicycle and takes about thirty minutes or so. There's free parking for those who are driving there.

Historical Highlights:

Mrs. Reid's piano and sheet music is still in the drawing room, and there's a newspaper in the sitting room that headlines the sinking of the Titanic. Also of note is a 1920's telephone in the study, and an 18th century French commode.

Dean says,

"If you like handmade furniture, old books, and historic personal furnishings then you'll really enjoy this place."

Andie says,

"If you happen to see a gentleman taking care of the ticketing just inside the front door it's probably David, one of the main caretakers of the place. If so, ask him about the resident ghost because he's actually seen and heard her. Others have also heard her ghostly footsteps."

Explore Score:

Ask to see the kitchens as you near the end of the tour. They are visited upon request only.

Stair Scare:

This stately home cannot accommodate those with limited mobility.

Treat Time:

Though there are light snacks and beverages offered for sale on the property, why not bring your own picnic? You're welcome to make yourself at home on any of the expansive lawns.

PART 3

[Skip it Unless it's Your Thing]

In Scotland, a graveyard or cemetery is called a Kirkyard

©Alán Duke

Greyfriars Kirkyard
[Edinburgh's most famous graveyard]

This *kirkyard* (Gaelic for "graveyard") in the center of town is extremely famous and is supposedly one of Edinburgh's top sights. This is probably because of its connection with a Skye Terrier named Bobby who stayed faithfully by his master's grave from 1857 to 1871; a Disney film was made about it in the 1960's. It's also the place where local author J. K. Rowling got several of her character names for her *Harry Potter* books — yes, right off the gravestones.

We find a visit here to be actually quite boring. Take a stroll through it if you must, perhaps on the way to Grassmarket Square which is nearby. If you've never been in an old cemetery, you might find it interesting. Many of the city's "ghost tours" use it as a gathering spot.

https://greyfriarskirk.com/visit-us/kirkyard

Free public space

Located at 26 Candlemaker Row
-in the Old Town, left of Greyfriars Bobby bar
Edinburgh

Intl. calling: (011) 44-131-225-1900 (Greyfriars Church)
Local mobile calling: 0-131-225-1900

Always open

Cultural Tidbit:

Some of the tombstone names in the Kirkyard that inspired J. K. Rowling are McGonagall, Moody, and Thomas Riddell (changed by the author to "Tom Riddle" who is of course, Lord Voldemort.

Dean says,

"Enter Greyfriars Kirkyard through the alleyway next to Greyfriars Bobby bar, located on George IV Bridge Street. You can't miss it, and you'll even see the bronze sculpture of Bobby, the Skye Terrier out front."

Andie says,

"Some of the larger tombs are very ornate and have sculpted angels."

No Stair Scare:

There are no stairs to worry about at the Kirkyard and the even paths through its different sections are smooth and accommodating to those with limited mobility.

The Scott Monument is an iconic symbol of the city

©Alán Duke

The Scott Monument
[Where literary fans get really high]

The gorgeous, two-hundred-foot Victorian-Gothic monument right off of Princes Street is hard to miss and you would have undoubtedly come upon it without our help. What you may not realize is that you can usually climb it... for a fee. By the way, it's not a monument to Scotsmen everywhere; it's a monument to the famous author, Sir Walter Scott. You can see his marble likeness (with his dog) right above the base. It's said to be one of the largest monuments to a writer in the world.

www.edinburghmuseums.org.uk/venue/scott-monument

Located at the intersection of Princes Street and St. David Street
-in the city center
Edinburgh

Intl. calling: (011) 44-131-529-4068
Local mobile calling: 0-131-529-4068

Cultural Tidbit:
The monument is decorated with little statues of more than sixty-four different characters from Scott's books.

Andie says,

"I have no problem with its entry being closed right now. Tight spaces and narrow stairways are just not my thing."

Dean says,

"It's fun to go to the top of it, and the views of the city below are spectacular."

Stair Scare:

Viewing the monument from the street or park is easy; climbing the 288 steps to the top is not. Obviously not suitable for those with limited mobility.

Arthur's Seat and Holyrood Park
[An ancient volcano provides a steep climb]

If you have a morning free or are an early riser, head over to Holyrood Park and climb to the top of Arthur's Seat. This hill is actually an extinct volcano and its formation is the highest point in all of Edinburgh at 823 feet. It offers a challenging hike and breathtaking views over the city. Fitness junkies, serious hikers, and nature lovers should rejoice and not miss it... this is Scottish wilderness, with a loch and all, right in the city center.

No official website

Free public park

Located in Holyrood Park
-in the Old Town, south of the Salisbury Crags
Edinburgh

Always open

Pro Tip:
No matter the season, be sure to take a few bottles of water and some energy snacks with you.

Dean says,
"While there are at least six different routes by which you can reach the summit of Arthur's Seat, the paths starting in the park area just south of the Palace of Holyroodhouse are the easiest hikes. Find Queen's Drive and head upward."

Andie says,

"The hike to the top and back will take about two hours to complete."

Explore Score:

See if you can find the ruins of a medieval abbey hidden within the park. And if you make your way to the hill's southern face, you'll see Duddingston Loch (lake) and its village below. Don't worry about getting lost because all paths either lead back to the Old Town or to Duddingston.

Historical Highlight:

Depending on whom you ask, this formation is said to be named after the legendary King Arthur and is a possible location of his Camelot Castle. Perhaps he isn't legendary after all.

Pic Click:

Take a selfie to prove you made it up there.

Stair Scare:

The natural incline of Arthur's Seat is steep, making this is an activity specifically for those who are in very good physical condition. It is not accommodating to those with limited mobility.

*The city museum has a multitude of artifacts
from old Edinburgh*

©*Alán Duke*

Museum of Edinburgh
[The city's own story, housed in a historic building]

Lovers of antiquities and 16th century houses will marvel at this little gem of a museum in the Canongate neighborhood. Positioned right on the Royal Mile, it's easy to find and can be explored in less than an hour. The collections here all relate to the origins and history of Edinburgh and provide a clearer understanding of this fantastic city. We like it for the rustic, historic building more than its items but if you're into city kitsch then check it out. It's free.

www.edinburghmuseums.org.uk/venue/museum-edinburgh

Free to enter
No pre-booking needed

Located at 142 Canongate (aka *the Royal Mile/ High Street)*
-in the Old Town
Edinburgh

Intl. calling: (011) 44-131-529-4143
Local mobile calling: 0-131-529-4143

Open daily
Closed on Christmas Day, December 26, New Year's Day, & January 2

Historical Highlight:
Objects from the city's past are lovingly displayed throughout the former Huntly House and part of the

Acheson House next door, both built in the 1500's. The structures are just as intriguing as the treasures they now hold.

Cultural Tidbits:

This museum displays a mind-blowing copy of the history-changing National Covenant of 1638, which led to their civil war. In a room upstairs, children will appreciate seeing the actual collar and bowl of Greyfriars *Bobby*, the Skye Terrier who stayed by his former master's gravesite for over a decade in Greyfriars Kirkyard.

Andie says,

"Both the museum and nearby Bakehouse Close were featured filming locations for the series *Outlander*. If you're a fan, walk into the alleyway *close* next door and spot Jamie Malcolm Fraser's print shop."

Stair Scare:

This old building cannot accommodate those with limited mobility.

Another wee dram of whisky please!

More? Well, there's the super historic, super famous, *super haunted* Tolbooth Tavern right across from the museum. It's open Thursday through Sunday only. Since it's too haunted to be open late into the night, its hours are from around 12:30pm to 7pm. Good luck!

*Camera Obscura is an unusual and
amusing place to visit*

©Alán Duke

Camera Obscura & World of Illusions
[Kids love discovering this interactive museum]

The Camera Obscura tourist attraction is one of those places where you either love it or don't love it. Kids will definitely be more impressed with it than adults, although people who possess a childlike curiosity will probably have a great time inside. Visual tricks with lights, mirrors, and spinning instruments are what make this place tick. Their most popular interactive experiences are the Vortex Tunnel, the Mirror Maze, and the perplexing Shrinking Room.

You can re-enter anytime on the same day for free to revisit something you liked or see something you missed the first time around. If you want to bond as a family over some unique experiences and have a few laughs at the same time, go for it.

www.camera-obscura.co.uk

Online bookings are recommended but not required

Located on Castle Hill
-in the Old Town, at the western end of the Royal Mile
Edinburgh

Intl. calling: (011) 44-131-226-3709
Local mobile calling: 0-131-226-3709

Open daily
Closed on Christmas Day

Andie says,

"This place may seem touristy and silly but it's actually a lot of fun."

Dean says,

"I love the *severed head on a table* illusion. It freaks me out!"

Pro Tip:

Their fascinating Camera Obscura Show is back and they are giving demonstrations of the device on fair weather days. This is included with admission.

Great Clue:

Most folks spend close to two hours inside this attraction.

Stair Scare:

This attraction cannot accommodate those with limited mobility.

Treat Time:

Afterwards, enjoy a creamy gelato at Mary's Milk Bar in Grassmarket Square. To get there quick, just take the stairs on the left side of the castle esplanade all the way down and then head to the right.

We're pretty sure this is the Scottish Gallery of Modern Art no. 2

©Alán Duke

Scottish National Galleries of Modern Art (No. 1 and No. 2)

[Modern art housed in two separate buildings]

Full disclosure: we're not great fans of modern art and are not easily impressed by it. We have chosen to include Edinburgh's two modern art galleries in our guide because there are plenty of people who love weird things, the weirder the better, so here goes…

Located right across from one another on the west side of town, Edinburgh's two modern art collections are housed in twin neoclassical buildings and feature bizarre works by both famous and lesser-known artists. Though these two buildings make a great first impression, the art inside of them pales in comparison to other modern art museums that we've seen.

www.nationalgalleries.org/visit/Scottish-national-gallery-modern-art

Free to enter
No pre-booking needed

Located at 73 & 75 Belford Road
-in the city center west
Edinburgh

Intl. calling: (011) 44-131-624-6200
Local mobile calling: 0-131-624-6200

Open daily
Closed on some major holidays

Pro Tip:

You can ride here on the Gallery Bus, a free shuttle servicing these two museums as well as the one with the classical collections (located on the Mound near Waverley Station.)

Andie says,

"Modern Two features an extensive collection of Dada and Surrealist art."

Mealtime Clue:

Both Modern One and Modern Two have excellent cafés featuring fresh food and baked goods made on the premises. If you need to eat, we recommend dining in them especially since there's nothing else good nearby at all.

No Stair Scare:

Both Modern One and Modern Two have elevators and are completely accessible for those with limited mobility.

Is this more of a museum for children? Could be.

©Alán Duke

National Museum of Scotland
[An eclectic place popular with families]

This "top sight in Edinburgh" might raise your expectations a bit high; after all, it's *the* National Museum of Scotland and will probably be filled with fascinating Scottish things that will bring your inner *outlander* into full expression. Well, not really.

While it does have some Scottish items in its vast collection, they are completely overwhelmed by everything else that is *not* Scottish. It has a curious curation that we simply don't understand... dinosaur bones, vintage fashions, cloisonné urns, replicas of airplanes, Egyptian jewelry, clocks, etc. And throughout it all are groups of uncontrolled hollering children running about.

Try to go on a quiet morning and just have a peek around. While some of it is quite interesting, we cannot fathom how the curators decided *what* to put *where*. You'll understand once you go inside.

www.nms.ac.uk

Free to enter
No pre-booking needed

Located on Chambers Street
-in the Old Town
Edinburgh

Intl. calling: (011) 44-300-123-6789
Local mobile calling: 0-300-123-6789

Open daily
Closed on Christmas Day

Historical Highlight:

An intriguing archaeological find is here… the famous Lewis chess pieces can be seen in the room called *Kingdom of the Scots.* Carved in Norway from walrus tusk in the late 12th century, they were found on a Scottish beach in 1831. This museum has a partial set because the British Museum in London has the rest.

Andie says,

"This museum has an elaborate traveling case of the Princess Borghese (sister of Napoleon) that I find to be exquisite. And their changing *special exhibits* are usually very well done."

Dean says,

"One of the most famous artifacts in the museum is the taxidermied remains of the cloned sheep, Dolly. At least she was actually Scottish."

Pro Tip:

If you want to see the highlights without the confusion, join one of their complimentary small-group guided tours. They are offered throughout the day for adults only.

No Stair Scare:

The museum is completely accessible to those with limited mobility.

Mealtime Clue:

The museum's casual Balcony Café overlooks the gorgeous Grand Gallery. It is open daily but does not accept cash.

Princes Street Gardens
and the Ross Fountain
[People-watching in the city's green space]

Whether it's a picnic location you're seeking or just a scenic spot to relax, the Princes Street Gardens is the place to be. This is the ultimate in city improvement; the disgusting *Nor Loch* lake beneath the Old Town that received the contents of all those chamber pots from the past was drained and cleaned up to build this park.

By 1820 it had become a glorious sight and continues to grow its collection of public monuments and memorials. These include the Scott monument, the David Livingstone statue, the Royal Scots Regimental Memorial, the Scots American War Memorial, and the Ross Fountain. Perhaps in response to its unsanitary history, the gardens now boast modern public toilets and even a play area for the kids. Find a bench and make it yours.

Free public park

Located along Princes Street
-in the city center, from Lothian Road to Waverley Station
Edinburgh

Open everyday from 7am to 5pm or later
Extended hours offered during the summer months

Historical Highlight:
The Ross Fountain is located at the western end of the gardens. Originally from 1872, it was restored just last year.

Hidden Gem:

The world-renowned Floral Clock is a planting at the eastern corner of the park near The Mound. It was first installed in 1903 and always commemorates a special anniversary of the city's history. The full display takes about 30,000 miniature plants and flowers.

Mealtime Clue:

The park has several ice cream and waffle kiosks as well as a casual eatery called The Fountain Café. At the other end of the park, you'll find The Scottish Café and Restaurant beneath the connecting area of the National Gallery of Classical Art and the Royal Scottish Academy. There are picnic tables near the Ross Fountain and hundreds of regular benches throughout the park where you can enjoy a packed lunch.

No Stair Scare:

Several of the entrances to the park are stair-free and therefore accessible to those with limited mobility.

PART 4
[Feasting]

Food Made With Love

Eating well in Edinburgh is easy and will be a major part of your experience here. It's suddenly a foodie town, and not expensive when you compare it to places like London or New York. But like all cities in the UK, it has its share of touristy spots where the food is not that great.

Some of the more famous Scottish specialties are divine and should be sought out while you're here. These include *bangers* (the word for any kind of sausage links,) *neeps and tatties* (turnips and potatoes mashed up together,) *cullen skink* (a creamy fish soup made from haddock and potatoes,) *Scotch pies* (lamb or other ground meat and spices inside a flaky crust,) *cranachan* (a decadent dessert made with fresh raspberries, cream, honey, whisky, and oats,) *haggis* (the ubiquitous 'ofal' treat made from all those other parts,) and of course Scotch whisky.

Edinburgh is a very international place and the food offerings here reflect it. Of course, you could eat only the traditional foods but you would be missing out on some really great restaurants. When we come here, we're ready to dine on the flavors of Spain, France, and Thailand as well as Scotland. Edinburgh boasts a huge weekend brunch scene and almost every restaurant now offers vegan and vegetarian dishes.

We'll help you sort it all out in this chapter. As usual, we're excited to clue you in on some of our specific favorites but whether you end up in one of our recommended eateries or not, follow this general guideline: if they offer a tourist menu then it's probably not where you'll find the best food. Don't worry because all the places listed here have delicious food made with love. And they are worth finding.

Andie says,

"Like in Europe, the shrimp served to you in restaurants here will be a goodly size but will almost always be presented on the plate complete with their eyes, tail, shell, and spindly leg things. If you're not used to this it can be off-putting. You can request that the chef peel it all off for you –some kitchens will comply and some won't."

Dean says,

"The service in Edinburgh is very friendly and reflects the overall mood of Scotland. Don't be afraid to ask your server what's good that day, and the price too if they recommend something that's not on their printed menu."

Our favorite meal in Edinburgh is at the humble Makars Mash

©Alán Duke

Makars Gourmet Mash Bar

The seemingly "simple" food being served at this cute but rustic restaurant is actually not simple at all. Superbly seasoned sausages and delicate, flavorful mashed potatoes topped with the perfect gravy come together to create our favorite dinner in all of Edinburgh. Oh that life was always this simple.

Makars is located in the city center (on the Mound) and offers hungry diners a variety of lip-smacking dishes using only locally sourced meats and produce. They are not fancy; you certainly don't have to get all dressed up for a meal there which is kind of reassuring.

Limited reservations online / Some tables held aside for walk-ins

www.gourmet-mash-bar.com

££-£££
Ambience: Modern rustic
Noise level: Medium
Lighting: Soft

Credit Cards: Yes
WiFi: No
Full bar
Accessible: Call ahead for current info

Located at 9 North Bank Street
-in the city center/ Old Town
Edinburgh

Intl. calling: (011) 44-131-226-1178
Local mobile calling: 0-131-226-1178

Open daily
Closed on major holidays so call ahead

Clothing Clue:

The dress code for this restaurant is casual to smart casual.

It's hard to decide which amazing tapas to order at Andaluz

©Alán Duke

Andaluz

When you crave a meal of great flavor and variety, go to Andaluz and order up a table full of tapas. Every one of their authentic Spanish dishes is more delicious than the next and together make for a very satisfying supper. We love the location on George Street in the New Town but they do have one in the Old Town as well. Try the seared green pimientos and a platter of thinly sliced Jamón ibérico. Heavenly!

Reservations recommended

www.cafeandaluz.com

£££
Ambience: Modern Spanish Patio
Noise level: Medium
Lighting: Dim

Credit Cards: Yes
WiFi: No
Full bar
Accessible: No

Located at 77 George Street
-in the New Town
Edinburgh

Intl. calling: (011) 44-131-220-9980
Local mobile calling: 0-131-220-9980

Open daily

The dress code for this restaurant is smart casual

Refined French cuisine is served at Escargot Bleu

©Alán Duke

Escargot Bleu

Where do locals like to go for a fine meal? You'll find many of them at Escargot Bleu where the authentic French cuisine is inspired by the freshest Local mobile produce. This lovely restaurant on a quiet residential street is decidedly away from the crowded tourist scene. We adore their seasonal dishes like rabbit with mustard sauce and their *bouillabaisse* is simply luscious. Try the *prix fix* menu for a top-notch meal at a relatively wee price.

Reservations required

www.lescargotbleu.co.uk

£££-££££
Ambience: Upscale French bistro
Noise level: Medium
Lighting: Soft

Credit Cards: Yes
WiFi: No
Full bar
Accessible: Call ahead

Located at 56 Broughton Street
-in the New Town
Edinburgh

Intl. calling: (011) 44-131-557-1600/ Local: 0-131-557-1600

Open Wednesday through Saturday only
Closed Sundays, Mondays, and some major holidays

The dress code for this restaurant is smart casual to a wee bit dressy.

Afternoon Tea at "Rhubarb" is almost a surreal experience

©Alán Duke

Rhubarb [at The Prestonfield House Hotel]

Wow, this is what we call a restaurant. Tucked inside a gorgeous manor house from the 1600's that has been transformed into a five-star hotel; Rhubarb is as good as it gets. Dining here will set you back a bit, though they do offer a prix fix menu that's relatively affordable. But what we really love here is their afternoon tea service. You get to choose from a dozen very special tea blends, some of which we've never seen anywhere else. Then a triple-tiered silver tray arrives carrying sandwiches, scones and pastries. Everything on it is tasty, even the haggis bonbons.

You can add champagne to this lovely feast to make it even more special. All this, plus a Michelin star and live peacocks wandering around out the window.

Reservations highly recommended

www.prestonfield.com/dine/rhubarb

£££-£££££

Ambience: Romantic 17th century manor house
Noise level: Soft
Lighting: Soft

Credit Cards: Yes
WiFi: Yes
Full bar
Accessible: Yes

Located on Priestfield Road
-in a southern section of the city, Edinburgh

Intl. calling: (011) 44-131-225-1333/Local: 0-131-225-1333
Open daily

Italian cuisine awaits you on historic Cockburn Street

La Locanda

Locals know where to go for the most authentic Italian food in Edinburgh and you'll see many of them dining here. This smallish restaurant located right on famous Cockburn Street prides itself on their chef's nightly specials made with seasonal ingredients and happens to have the tastiest *arancini* balls this side of the Mediterranean. La Locanda serves up great Bolognese-style lasagna, and offers many other familiar dishes. While they are open for breakfast, serving the usual basic Scottish offerings, we recommend this place for its Italian lunch or dinner.

Reservations highly recommended

www.lalocandaedinburgh.co.uk

££-£££
Ambience: Modern Italian *trattoria*
Noise level: Medium
Lighting: Standard

Credit Cards: Yes
WiFi: Yes
Beer and wines
Accessible: Yes

Located at 61 Cockburn Street
-in the Old Town, just off the Royal Mile, Edinburgh

Intl. calling: (011) 44-131-622-7447/Local: 0-131-622-7447

Open daily
Call ahead for hours on major holidays

The Mussel and Steak Bar

For a scrumptious meal right in Grassmarket Square you can't beat the popular Mussel and Steak Bar. Their huge bucket of rope-grown Scottish mussels is the main draw here but don't worry if they're not your thing; there are plenty of other offerings and creative side dishes, one of which is a macaroni and cheese that will knock your socks off. Come early to avoid the crowds because reservations are only accepted during the off-season months.

Reservations necessary during the high season

www.musselandsteakbar.com

££-££££
Ambience: Modern upscale bistro
Noise level: Loud
Lighting: Standard

Credit Cards: Yes
WiFi: Yes
Full bar
Accessible: Yes

Located at 110 Grassmarket Square, at Bow Street
-in the Old Town
Edinburgh

Intl. calling: (011) 44-131-225-5028
Local mobile calling: 0-131-225-5028

Open daily
Call ahead for hours on major holidays

Even the appetizers are beautiful at Chaophraya

©Alán Duke

Chaophraya Thai

Edinburgh has several old school Thai restaurants but this is not one of them. Chaophraya (pronounced *chow-fry-uh*) is where locals go for a special meal or birthday celebration. This spacious restaurant serves creative dishes and fancy cocktails on the upper level of a modern building in the New Town. We love to sit on their terrace balcony and nibble on an appetizer platter.

Try one of their tangy Tamarind dishes or savor a bowl of green curry. While relatively well-priced to begin with, their lunch specials offer a terrific deal. We find that Thai food is a great dining alternative when you've tired of the traditional fare.

Reservations recommended

https://chaophraya.co.uk/edinburgh

££-££££
Ambience: Elegant modern Thai
Noise level: Medium
Lighting: Dim

Credit Cards: Yes
WiFi: Yes
Full bar
Accessible: Yes

Located at 33 Castle Street
(4th floor via elevator)
-*in the New Town*, Edinburgh

Intl. calling: (011) 44-131-634-2300/ *Local: 0-131-634-2300*

Open daily
Call ahead for hours on major holidays

The OX

A "Sunday roast" is a tradition in Scotland, and one of the best for the money can be found at The OX. If you're going to be in town over a weekend, book a table here for Sunday evening and get ready for their special menu featuring slow-cooked roast beef with real Yorkshire pudding and gravy. They have other roasts as well, like lamb or pork belly, and all come with potatoes, leeks, and other veggies.

Reservations recommended

www.theoxedinburgh.com

££-£££
Ambience: Old world wooden interiors
Noise level: Medium
Lighting: Soft

Credit Cards: Yes
WiFi: No
Full bar
Accessible: Yes

Located at 49-51 London Street
-in the New Town, near Broughton Street
Edinburgh

Intl. calling: (011) 44-131-556-9808/ Local: 0-131-556-9808

Open daily
Call ahead for hours on major holidays

For a *Sunday Roast* in the Old Town instead, check out the 17th century Doric Tavern on Market Street.
Call 0-131-225-1084."

The Kitchin (Michelin-starred)

For an extraordinary meal in Leith, especially when visiting the Royal Yacht Britannia, make a reservation at The Kitchin. Chef Tom Kitchin is widely known as a culinary wizard and oversees things personally at this his namesake restaurant that he and his wife opened in 2006. Award-winning dishes will surprise and delight you here, where you'll be surrounded by lovely interiors and refined service. It's the best of Scottish ingredients paired with a very French technique and style.

Reservations recommended

https://thekitchin.com

£££ - ££££
Ambience: Modern chic
Noise level: Low
Lighting: Soft

Credit Cards: Yes
WiFi: Yes
Full bar
Accessible: Yes

Located at 78 Commercial Quay
-in the neighborhood of Leith
Edinburgh

Intl. calling: (011) 44-131-555-1755/ Local: 0-131-555-1755

Open Tuesday through Saturday
Closed Sundays and Mondays, and from December 23 to January 12

PART 5
[Breakfast, Lunch & Treats]

Plus Pastries
& Local Favorites

American fast-food eateries are abundant here, but that's not why you came to Scotland. Instead, try one of our recommended cafés for a delicious breakfast or lunch because a truly different experience will make your Edinburgh visit truly memorable. After these we list our favorite pastry shops and other goodies...

The Pantry
Fresh eggs and fluffy waffles make for a great brunch

Fresh, local produce is the inspiration for the food in this tiny restaurant near the elegant Royal Circus street in the New Town. If you're a sucker for creative benedicts or thick, fluffy Belgian waffles with fresh fruit, don't miss it. These dishes are served up all day, every day along with several lunch offerings like homemade soup or slow-cooked cassoulet. Delicious!

Reservations not taken

www.thepantryedinburgh.co.uk

Located at 1 NW Circus Place
-in the New Town
Edinburgh

Intl. calling: (011) 44-131-629-0206
Local mobile calling: 0-131-629-0206

Open daily for breakfast and lunch
Closed on some major holidays so call ahead

Accessible: No

French Toast with fresh rhubarb at The Larder

©Alán Duke

The Edinburgh Larder

The Edinburgh Larder owns two restaurants next door to each other. Make sure you go to the larger one, not the tiny one called *Little Larder* unless you want something simple like porridge. The main Larder has a lovely farmhouse interior and is tops when you want a full breakfast. Locals claim it has the best black pudding in town. We like their eggy French toast with seasonal fruits and rich clotted cream.

Reservations recommended so call ahead for a table.

www.edinburghlarder.co.uk

Located at 15 Blackfriars Street
-in the Old Town, within the eastern part of the Royal Mile
Edinburgh

Intl. calling: (011) 44-131-556-6922
Local mobile calling: 0-131-556-6922

Open daily for breakfast and lunch
Open all day until 10pm on Fridays and Saturdays

Accessible: Yes

At Mums it's all about slow food

©Alán Duke

Mums Great Comfort Food
Casual home cooking offered all day long

When nothing but a plate of steak-and-ale stew will do, come as you are to Mum's Great Comfort Food. This casual, retro eatery is a favorite of twenty-somethings in the Old Town and serves up hearty recipes like your Scottish grandma used to make when she was sober. Stews, meat pies, bangers and mash are all on the menu. We like their giant cheeseburgers too. Mum's is open for breakfast, lunch, and dinner, making it the perfect place to bring your hungry kids.

www.monstermashcafe.co.uk

Located at 4 Forrest Road
-in the Old Town
Edinburgh

Intl. calling: (011) 44-131-260-9806
Local mobile calling: 0-131-260-9806

Open daily
Closed on some major holidays

Accessible: Yes

The Grand Café
Late-night dining in the Scotsman Hotel

Since 1905, this restaurant has thrived. They offer a full brunch menu every single day and have an ambience that can make any meal seem special. It's part of the historic Scotsman Hotel but does have its own street entrance too. The service is unhurried and the atmosphere is comfortable yet elegant, with live jazz or piano at night. Reserve at least a week ahead to get a table for the weekend. Though we love it for its scrumptious Afternoon Tea, the Grand Café is one of the few restaurants in town that's open for late-night dining and drinks.

http://grandcafeedinburgh.co.uk

Located at 20 North Bridge
-in the city center
Edinburgh

Intl. calling: (011) 44-131-622-2999
Local mobile calling: 0-131-622-2999

Open Sunday through Thursday until 11pm
Open Fridays and Saturdays until 1am

Accessible: Call ahead for the most current info

Oink

Pulled pork doesn't get more real than this. Even though Oink has a few locations in the city center, each one gets an entire hog in the window every day. This is where your sandwich will come from, moist and savory, and topped with your choice of stuffing, sauces, and crispy crackling. The sandwiches come in three sizes to fit any appetite. Slow roasting the hog for hours gives this pulled pork a tender bite. Go get one! (Counter service only)

www.oinkhogroast.co.uk

Located at 34 Victoria Street
-in the Old Town
Edinburgh

Intl. calling: (011) 44-777-196-8233
Local mobile calling: 0-777-196-8233

Open daily for lunch
Closed on some major holidays

Accessible: Call ahead

Traditional Swedish rolls are just some of the surprising things you'll find in Edinburgh

©Kanel Bullar

Breads and Pastries

Söderberg Bakery

Authentic Swedish sweet rolls freshly baked in Scotland? Why not? This is an international city and Söderberg Bakery is part of the fun. We enjoy these yeasty babies with a cappuccino and call it breakfast. There are several locations in both the Old Town and the New Town, but their shop near the entrance of Dean Village makes it the perfect place to stop on our way to the gnomes and faeries.

www.soderberg.uk/the-bakery-1

Located at 31 Queensferry Street
-in the city center west, near Dean Village
Edinburgh

Intl. calling: (011) 44-131-225-8286
Local mobile calling: 0-131-225-8286

Open daily
Closed on some major holidays so call ahead

Accessible: Yes

Everyone loves a cake or croissant from Valerie

©Alán Duke

Patisserie Valerie

We like the variety of goodies at Patisserie Valerie and whether you're after a light breakfast or a sweet pastry in the afternoon, you'll always find fair prices and real freshness here because their breads and pastries are all baked on the premises. There are three locations around the city; in the New Town, in the Old Town, and on North Bridge (just off the Royal Mile.) We love the located one on quaint, pedestrianized Rose Street, but they're all great.

www.patisserie-valerie.co.uk

Located at 158 Rose Street
-in the New Town
Edinburgh

Intl. calling: (011) 44-131-220-1336
Local mobile calling: 0-131-220-1336

Open daily
Closed on some major holidays so call ahead

Accessible: Yes

Local cheeses are the standouts at IJ Mellis

©Alán Duke

I J Mellis Cheesemongers

Your cheese dreams can and will come true at I. J. Mellis. They have a gorgeous shop in the Old Town that's just brimming with the best farmhouse cheeses from Scotland and beyond. They have everything you could possibly want as well as some things you've probably never heard of. Be sure to have them seal your cheese purchase in plastic if you plan on bringing it back to the U.S. (Meats are <u>not</u> allowed through customs, even if cured *and* sealed in plastic.)

Their enviable location smack dab on Victoria Street is near those Oink piggy sandwiches. There's another location as well, on Baker Street in the New Town. Ask one of the friendly staff members for a taste of whatever catches your eye.

https://mellischeese.net

Located at 6 Victoria Street
-in the Old Town
Edinburgh

Intl. calling: (011) 44-131-226-6215
Local mobile calling: 0-131-226-6215

Open daily
Closed on some major holidays so call ahead

Accessible: Yes

They make their candy right in front of you
at the Fudge Kitchen

©Alán Duke

Fudge Kitchen

Readers of *Clued In Travel Books* know how much we love homemade fudge and the Fudge Kitchen is our favorite in both England and Scotland. Luckily, there's a convenient location right on the Royal Mile. Try the dark chocolate mint or butterscotch fudge. (They even have vegan choices.) Enjoy a bit now *and* bring some home. Win, win!

https://fudgekitchen.co.uk

Located at 30 High Street
-in the eastern part of the Royal Mile
Edinburgh

Intl. calling: (011) 44-131-558-1517
Local mobile calling: 0-131-558-1517

Open daily
Closed on some major holidays so call ahead

Accessible: Yes

Haggis - *The local favorite, if you dare*

If there's one food item that can be called *the most Scottish* it has to be haggis. It is literally found everywhere here. Bars, fine restaurants, casual lunch counters, and even gift shops flaunt its presence, often with a wee handwritten sign at the entrance. Even the exquisite, formal afternoon tea service at Rhubarb (in the Prestonfield House Hotel) includes it on their tiered silver tray as Haggis bonbons. *What?*

From the haggis we've sampled, those bonbons are the winners. While we're not great fans of this local delicacy, its importance to the city's history as a food staple cannot be overstated.

So, what is haggis? It's a mixture of oats, pepper, spices, suet, and ofal boiled in a bag made of stomach lining. What is *ofal*? It's the parts of an animal not usually preferred, like heart, stomach, windpipe, intestine, and feet. Try it with a side of *neeps and tatties* (turnips and potatoes.)

Even though you can find it everywhere, our solid recommendation is to head over to 48 Cockburn Street, just off the Royal Mile, to try it at *Arcade Haggis & Whisky House.* People seem to agree that it's the best.

PART 6
[Pubs & Booze]

Our Haunted Pub Crawl

Edinburgh's sinister history and preserved medieval town has given it a reputation as one of the most haunted cities in the world. Indeed, there are so many places deemed haunted that it's difficult to keep track of them all but one thing is sure...many of them are pubs. That's why we just couldn't resist sending you on a haunted pub crawl. And like any good crawl, all four of our picks are in one area.

Unlike London, Edinburgh's pubs are open late, sometimes even after midnight on the weekends. Enjoy that whisky but keep your senses about ye 'cause ye never know what be lurkin' thar in the corner. *Slanjevah!*

Our haunted pub crawl starts here, at the White Hart Inn

©Alán Duke

The White Hart Inn – *for a chilling good start*

Ask any Edinburgher which pub is the *most* haunted and all will say this one is. That's why it tops our haunted pub crawl... if you don't make it to the others at least you can say you had a drink and survived the infamous White Hart Inn. Established in 1556, it's also the oldest pub in the city and has experienced unexplained occurrences for centuries. The staff there is terrified of its cellar. Bonus: they offer live, traditional Scottish music almost every night for no extra charge.

www.belhavenpubs.co.uk/pubs/midlothian/white-hart

Located at 34 Grassmarket Square
-in the Old Town
Edinburgh

Intl. calling: (011) 44-131-226-2806
Local mobile calling: 0-131-226-2806

Open daily
Call ahead for hours on major holidays

Accessible: Yes

* * *

The Beehive Inn - *Will the real Ebenezer please stand up?*

Now move west a few yards and find The Beehive Inn. As a former coaching inn from the 17th century, it's one of the larger pubs in the area and has modern, renovated interiors. It once had cells for condemned prisoners who were to be hung in the square. Look for the historic "prisoner's cell door" that's still in place near the stairs.

When Dickens was visiting Edinburgh in 1841, he noticed a kirkyard gravestone from the 1700's that was carved *Ebenezer Scroggie – a meal man* (meaning that he was a corn merchant) but Dickens misread it and thought it said *a mean man*. He was strangely preoccupied by the memory of it, and wondering what made the man deserve such a terrible headstone. He figured the man had to have been absolutely despicable. This was the basis of one of his most famous characters, Ebenezer Scrooge from *A Christmas Carol.*

No one knows much about Ebenezer Scroggie (the corn merchant) except that he lived in the rooms just above the Beehive Inn.

During the warmer months the Beehive offers both indoor and outdoor seating thanks to its huge "secret garden" in the rear. Enjoy a table in the very shadow of Edinburgh Castle!

www.belhavenpubs.co.uk (shared website)

Located at 18 Grassmarket Square
-in the Old Town
Edinburgh

Intl. calling: (011) 44-131-225-7171
Local mobile calling: 0-131-225-7171

Open daily
Call ahead for hours on major holidays

Accessible: Yes

* * *

The infamous Last Drop Pub gives us the creeps

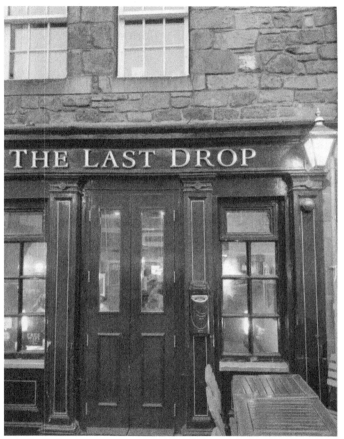

©Alán Duke

The Last Drop – *Why is that child in here?*

Next, head east in Grassmarket Square and look for the black exterior of The Last Drop. This pub used to stand next to gallows for public executions by hanging, an especially popular thing during the 18th century. The pub's name comes from those prisoners literally having their *last drop*.

This cozy establishment has several photos and nooses indicating its gruesome past, as well as a "resident female ghost." A young girl has been seen on numerous occasions and is known to play tricks on just about anyone inside. The Last Drop is also known for its vast collection of authentic cask ales. Yum!

www.nicholsonspubs.co.uk (shared website)

Located at 74 Grassmarket Square
-in the Old Town
Edinburgh

Intl. calling: (011) 44-131-225-4851
Local mobile calling: 0-131-225-4851

Open daily
Call ahead for hours on major holidays

Accessible: Yes

* * *

The Bow Bar - *Time to kick up your heels*

Exiting out the east side of Grassmarket Square, you'll need to head up West Bow Street, that gentle curving hill on your left that becomes Victoria Street. (We're trying to be gentle and exacting here because you've probably had more than a few drams of whisky by now and may not be as quick to understand.)

As you walk up the street you should notice The Bow Bar on your right. Go inside and grab a seat at the bar; this is the final stop of your crawl. It's the least fancy of the four we've chosen but if you're properly tipsy you may not notice. They have no food, no live music, and no garden. This is where young locals come to drink and mingle... that's it. We can't vouch for how haunted this one is but at this point it shouldn't matter to you. It was recently voted Scotland's Pub of the Year, probably because of their astounding two-hundred-fifty different malt beers.

www.thebowbar.co.uk

Located at 80 West Bow
-in the Old Town
Edinburgh

Intl. calling: (011) 44-131-226-7667
Local mobile calling: 0-131-226-7667

Open daily
Call ahead for hours on major holidays

Accessible: Yes

PART 7

[Edinburgh International Festival]

A Massive Festival
Unlike any Other!

The importance and sheer size of the city's annual International Festival cannot be overstated. For many visitors, this is *the* reason to come to Edinburgh. It's traditionally held during the month of August and includes offshoots of the original that have come into their own, namely the Fringe Festival and the Military Tattoo. Let us explain...

Conceived of by opera director Sir Rudolf Bing in the months following the end of WWII, it was his hope that an international festival would "heal the wounds of war through the languages of the arts." Edinburgh was chosen by Bing and the festival was born. It has continued and grown every year since.

Today, by special invitation from the current director, the International Festival brings together famous, first-class performers of classical music, theatre, opera, and dance from all around the globe. It also includes visual art exhibitions, special talks, and even workshops.

Over the years, smaller theatrical groups, comedy acts, contemporary musicians, and buskers who were not necessarily invited began to appear and enjoyed great admiration by the audiences already in attendance. This became the Fringe Festival which still takes place during the main International Festival. If counted by the number of acts, it's even larger than its high-brow cousin. A similar thing happened when some military bands joined in; now known as the Military Tattoo, it has grown to such a degree that there are now spectacular performances of military and piping bands from the world over that perform nightly during the festival. Along with a concurrent International Book Festival, the city has held more than 2,500 performances *a day*. Every possible venue is involved, even in the harbor suburb of Leith.

Tickets and information can be found online or at The Hub, a deconsecrated church at the edge of Castle Rock that has folks handling the entire thing. Note that many events, like the Military Tattoo, must be booked months in advance.

With all four of these organizations holding simultaneous events each August, this has become the largest festival in the world and is obviously a major draw for the city. There's even an opening ceremony and closing fireworks. Watch hotel rates double during this time. Even so, a visit to Edinburgh during the International Festival will provide lifelong memories to cherish. Come for the high arts, come for eclectic music and modern dance, come to smile at a juggler or hear your favorite author... just come.

The Hub
(Festival headquarters)

Intl. calling: (011) 44-131-473-2000
Local mobile calling: 0-131-473-2000

International Festival website:
www.eif.co.uk

Fringe Festival website:
www.edfringe.com

Military Tattoo website:
www.edintattoo.co.uk

International Book Festival website:
www.edbookfest.co.uk

PART 8

[Accommodations]

Hotels to Set the Mood

Where you stay will set the mood for your entire visit, even if you don't end up spending much time there. Just leaving from, or returning to, a beautiful hotel gives the traveler an indescribable feeling. We recommend first-time visitors to Edinburgh stay in the city center (be it old town or new town) in a neighborhood that really appeals to them.

Edinburgh has hundreds of hotels, many of which are relatively inexpensive when compared to London. We appreciate the services that a nice hotel can give you, and adore ones that boast a grand lobby. Finding one like that here is not easy, but it can be done. Remember, you'll always snag a better price in the off-season and hotel prices here will definitely rise during the International Festival. Whatever you choose, make sure it will set the right mood. It's where you'll start and end your day.

Pro Tip:

The star ratings shown are not generated by a consensus of "opinions." They are a strict *industry* rating, based on a particular hotel's offered guest services and capabilities. For instance, two similar hotels can be rated 3 stars or 4 stars depending if one has a restaurant. This system is meant to help you choose a hotel with the level of service and amenities you desire.

*The historic Scotsman Hotel sits between the
Medieval and Georgian neighborhoods*

©Alán Duke

The Scotsman Hotel (4 Stars)

The Scotsman could actually be the beginning and the end of this chapter because it's our favorite. If you like modern styling combined with old world service in the very center of town then this is your place. At the very edge of the Old Town and the New Town, it's a short walk or taxi ride to everything in Edinburgh. Named for the famous newspaper that once occupied its historic building, The Scotsman offers all the amenities that make a hotel special.

No two of their charming rooms are the same, which is very cool, and they regularly offer great specials through their website. As with all Edinburgh hotels, the price for a room in November will double in August.

-Located near Waverley Station
-Restaurant and bar
-24-hour room service
-Complimentary coffee and tea
-Smoke free
-Seventy-two guest rooms
Not Accessible

https://scotsmanhotel.co.uk

££-££££
Located at 20 North Bridge
-in the city center
Edinburgh

Intl. calling: (011) 44-131-556-5565
Local mobile calling: 0-131-556-5565

This hotel can be emailed directly through the website above.

The mysterious Witchery Hotel is in a class by itself

©Alán Duke

The Witchery by the Castle (5 Stars)

This Gothic-style hotel is one of a kind. Located on the spot where hundreds of the city's witches were burned in the 1600's, it offers just nine uniquely themed suites for couples only (and no children.) Amenities like champagne and a sumptuous breakfast are the norm here, and you might not want to leave your rooms once you settle in. It's romantic to a fault and boasts an opulent restaurant of velvet and candlelight.

There's no actual lobby but they do have a garden on the property. Best of all, you get bragging rights that your Edinburgh hotel is literally on Castle Rock.

-Opulent suites with four poster beds
-Located near Edinburgh Castle
-Michelin starred restaurant
-Complimentary breakfast hamper, or by candlelight in their dining room
-Complimentary champagne and cookies
-Old-fashioned roll top baths that fit two
-Smoke free property
-Nine unique guest suites
Not accessible

www.thewitchery.com

£££-£££££

Located at 352 Castlehill / Royal Mile
-in the Old Town, on the Edinburgh Castle esplanade

Intl. calling: (011) 44-131-225-5613
Local mobile calling: 0-131-225-5613
Email: info@thewitchery.com

A modern, glam vibe can be found at the landmark Hotel Caledonian

©Alán Duke

The Caledonian (5 Stars)

The historic building that is now owned by Hilton used to be the fabulous Caledonian Train Station and Hotel. It has been transformed into a world class hotel that offers everything you could want in an accommodation. The Caley, as it is still called today, sits at the end of the city's best shopping and is near the entrance of Dean Village. If you want top amenities but also need to be close to nature and the Water of Leith, choose this one for your stay.

-Located near Dean Village and city boutiques
-Two restaurants and two cocktail lounges
-Indoor swimming pool and whirlpool
-Award-winning spa
-Fitness center
-Accessible
-Two-hundred forty-one guest rooms

www.hilton.com/en/hotels/ednchqq-the-caledonian-edinburgh

££-£££££

Located on Princes Street, at Lothian Road
-in the city center west
Edinburgh

Intl. calling: (011) 44-131-222-8888
Local mobile calling: 0-131-222-8888

This hotel can be emailed directly through the website above.

Intimate old world charm is the essence of The George

©Alán Duke

The George - *Intercontinental Edinburgh*
(5 Stars)

The George hotel has a lot of charm. Its columned lobby and kilt-wearing doormen make you feel happy that you chose it for your accommodations. This neoclassical building used to be five townhouses belonging to the well-to-do of days gone by. It's been a hotel since 1881 but its rooms have been renovated to modern standards and appointed with a contemporary Scottish style.

-Charming, renovated rooms
-Restaurant and a café
-Late night bar
-Located near Waverley Station and the Portrait -Gallery
-Fitness center
-Accessible
-Two-hundred forty guest rooms

www.ihg.com/intercontinental/content/us/en/hotels-resorts

££-£££

Located at 19 George Street
-in the New Town
Edinburgh

Intl. calling: (011) 44-131-225-1251
Local mobile calling: 0-131-225-1251

This hotel can be emailed directly through the website above.

*The affordable Leonardo Boutique Hotel
lies south of the city center*

©Alán Duke

Leonardo Edinburgh City (3 Stars)

Leonardo Hotels offer fair prices for simple, modern rooms throughout the UK and their Edinburgh location is no exception. Situated south of the city center, its neighborhood is quiet and residential and is walkable to the main sights of the Scottish capital. Stay here if you require less expensive accommodations and like to be away from the noise of the city. It is well-maintained and does offer a full breakfast. Look for Lauriston Place and then enter on the side of the building through a courtyard, where some parking is available.

-Clean, modern rooms
-Near the University of Edinburgh
-Bar, open late
-Breakfast buffet
-Non-smoking property
-Accessible
-Fifty-two guest rooms, some are family-sized

www.leonardohotels.co.uk
(search Edinburgh City hotel)

££

Located at 79 Lauriston Place
(Entrance on Lauriston Park Road)
-south of the city center
Edinburgh

Intl. calling: (011) 44-131-622-7979
Local mobile calling: 0-131-622-7979
Email contact available directly through their website

*The enormous clock of the Balmoral Hotel
is a city landmark*

©Alán Duke

The Balmoral Hotel (5 Stars)

The palatial Victorian building at No. 1 Princes Street has been a hotel and meeting place in Edinburgh since 1902. Today it's no different, unless you count its £23 million renovation. This is the granddaddy of all Edinburgh hotels and is where you should stay if you can afford it. Rates during the warmer months are steep, but drop sharply in off-season months like November. See if you can snag a deal but remember timing is everything.

-Elegant lobby and reception area
-Two restaurants
-Cocktail bar and a whisky bar
-Award-winning afternoon tea
-Indoor swimming pool
-Full spa
-Fitness center and saunas
-Near Waverley Station
-Accessible
-One-hundred eighty-eight guest rooms

www.roccofortehotels.com/hotels-and-resorts/the-balmoral-hotel

££-£££££

Located at 1 Princes Street
-in the city center
Edinburgh

Intl. calling: (011) 44-131-556-2414
Local mobile calling: 0-131-556-2414

Email: reservations.balmoral@roccofortehotels.com

Opulent interiors and live peacocks define the gorgeous
Prestonfield House Hotel

©Alán Duke

Prestonfield House Edinburgh (5 Stars)

We wish we lived here. The Prestonfield is an elegant manor house situated within twenty acres of gardens south of Holyrood Park and Arthur's Seat. As a hotel, however, we feel it's a wee bit far from the city center to be convenient. Having said that, if you want the quiet Scottish countryside around you and don't mind paying for taxis or car services then this is your hotel. It provides gracious accommodations away from the crowds. And a real bargain can be had here in the off-season.

-Near Arthur's Seat
-*Rhubarb* restaurant, and four cocktail lounges
-Rooftop terrace
-Complimentary full breakfast
-In-room laptop-sized safe
-Smoke free property
-Accessible rooms available
-Twenty-three guest rooms

www.prestonfield.com

££-£££££

Located on Priestfield Road
-south of the city center
Edinburgh
A ten minute drive from Edinburgh Castle

Intl. calling: (011) 44-131-225-7800
Local mobile calling: 0-131-225-7800

Email: reservations@prestonfield.com

PART 9

[All Transport]

Airport Transfers
Taxis
Buses
& Train Stations

Whether you arrive by car, train, or airplane, we have a solution to get you to your accommodation without a hassle. Even though Edinburgh's airport is not far from the city center, your transportation choices matter. Read on to find the solution that's just right for you.

The nearest airport is EDI (Edinburgh International Airport) and boasts a large, modern terminal. It's about eight miles from the city center which means this is one of those rare destinations where we happily take an airport bus to *and* from. The popular Airlink Express Bus 100 is comfortable, fast, and has dedicated places for your luggage. In addition, it's so cheap that you barely have to budget it in. Check the section following for more details. Remember, if you're traveling with other people then it might pay to just take a taxi to your accommodations. The city's maximum number of passengers allowed in one taxi is five and all of them can accommodate wheelchairs. The website below is very handy if you need additional help.

The Edinburgh Airport's official website is:

www.edinburghairport.com

*The Airlink Bus 100 arrives every thirty minutes
and is very affordable*

©Alán Duke

Getting from the airport
to Edinburgh

Hire an Uber with your smart phone.

Cost is around £22 and they will pick you up outside
the terminal on the ground floor at the Pick-Up Zone
near the multi-level car park.

Grab a taxi from the queue outside baggage claim.

Cost is around £25 metered fare, depending on traffic.
Luggage handling will add a few extra pounds to your
total. Travel time is about twenty-five minutes.

Take the Airlink Bus.

Cost is around £6 one way / £8 round trip.

We can't say enough about the Lothian "Airlink Bus
100." It runs between the airport and the city center
and you can find them right outside the terminal.
Disembark at any stop you like along the route. The
city center stops are *Haymarket*, *West End*, *Princes Street*,
and *Waverley Bridge* (which is also the central train
station.) It ends at *St. Andrew Square*.

You can pay the bus driver exact change in pounds,
buy a ticket online in advance, or use a credit card in
one of the nearby ticketing machines. The entire trip is
less than thirty minutes long and discounts are offered
for children and for purchasing a return trip. These
buses run every thirty minutes everyday until
midnight, except Christmas Day.

*A note to visitors staying near the city's famous
Grassmarket Square: Do not disembark at the Haymarket station
by mistake; many first-time visitors confuse the two names.*

Hire an Airport Minivan.

Cost is around £30 metered fare, depending on traffic. *Luggage handling will add a few extra pounds to your total.* Travel takes about twenty-five minutes. These handy vehicles can take up to eight passengers (and all their luggage) for the same price as a taxi! Pre-book by calling internationally (011) 44-131-555-5555, or locally 0-131-555-5555.

Think twice before choosing the Edinburgh Tram.

The city's sleek, modern "light rail" tram system offers service between the airport and the city center but takes longer than the bus, costs more than the bus, and is farther from the airport terminal once you get there. (The folks who prefer it live in the outer suburbs of Edinburgh where the tram has stops that are most convenient for them.)

Getting from Edinburgh,
back to the airport

Hire an Uber with your smart phone.

Cost is around £25 and they will drop you off right at the airport terminal.

Grab a taxi from the queue outside baggage claim.

Cost is around £40 metered fare, depending on traffic. *Luggage handling will add a few extra pounds to your total.* Travel takes about twenty-five minutes.

Take the Airlink Bus.

Cost is around £6 one way / £8 round trip

The "Airlink Bus 100" runs frequently between the city center and the EDI airport. You can find them lined up on *Waverley Bridge* or at stops on *Princes Street*, *West End*, and the *Haymarket* station.

You can pay the bus driver in exact change in pounds or buy a ticket online in advance. The entire trip is about thirty minutes long. A discount is offered for children, and for purchasing a return trip. Buses run every thirty minutes until around midnight every day except Christmas Day.

Think twice before choosing the Edinburgh Tram.

The city's modern "light rail" offers service between the city center and the airport but takes longer, costs more, and drops off farther from the airport terminal.

From the train station
to your accommodations

If you're arriving in Edinburgh by train from another city, you may also have to take a taxi to get to your hotel or private apartment. They are easily found outside the Waverley rail station at taxi ranks on both the west and south sides. Always take the ones that have a roof light and refuse anyone offering you a ride in a private vehicle. Know where your accommodation is located in relationship to your arrival station, which could be *Waverley* or *Haymarket*.

Note: Taxis have a timed, metered fare but may charge a supplemental fee for the handling of your luggage. Find out more on our page titled *Taxi Clues*.

Main railway stations:

Edinburgh Waverley (city center)
Haymarket (smaller, accessing the west side)

Arriving in Edinburgh by Car:

Some travelers arrive in Edinburgh by rental car because they intend to see more of Scotland while they're here. That's okay, just expect to run into traffic during the high season and be prepared to ditch your vehicle at one of the city center car garages while you're in Edinburgh. Some hotels have deals with private garages to accommodate their guests so be sure to ask.

Regarding Uber around Town:

Uber is alive and well in Edinburgh and happens to be relatively well-priced.

Edinburgh's official taxi cabs come in many colors
so look for the roof light

©Alán Duke

Taxi Clues

First clue: only hire the city's official, metered taxis displaying a lit roof light. They come in all colors and shapes, so it's these roof lights that will distinguish them. Young Scots at the airport will sometimes approach people and claim they are taxi drivers. They may even try to help with your luggage. Just say no to them and head for the official taxi queue. Use your common sense. They're just trying to make some extra money with their own vehicles but are unlicensed and therefore unusable.

You can hail a taxi from anywhere as long as it's not too near an official taxi rank. They must be "available" of course, with their roof light lit up.

Edinburgh is a sprawling city so unless you prefer to hire an Uber, you'll probably need a taxi at some point. Note the following:

- Taxi queues are called taxi *ranks* by the local Scots

- Most taxi fares within central Edinburgh range between £10 to £15 and tipping is not necessary. It's appropriate to round up to the nearest pound, especially if the driver was helpful. The taxis usually accept credit cards, but always have cash on you in case their credit machine isn't functioning or can't find a signal. There's an additional 5% added to any taxi fare paid with plastic.

- Do not expect cab drivers to change a £50 or £100 note; they are not required to.

- If a taxi is called to your hotel or restaurant, it will already have its meter running from when it started to come get you. Don't be alarmed by this as it's completely legit and is the norm.

- Official taxi ranks can be found near main squares or sights, so note where they are in your area is case you ever need one quickly.

If you need to call a taxi, here are some local companies:

Central Taxis: 0-131-229-2468
Lida Taxi: 0-131-339-1399
E & I Taxis: 0-131-554-6775

Edinburgh Waverley is the city's most central train station

©Alán Duke

Train Clues

- Edinburgh's most active train station is *Edinburgh Waverley* and is where most people arrive or depart to other cities in Scotland or beyond.

- The self-ticketing machines are simple to use if you take your time. If you feel more comfortable getting your tickets from a human (or have questions to ask) you can always buy them at one of the ticket windows in the ticketing lounge.

- If you're holding a printed train ticket of any kind in Scotland, it will *automatically* be validated for use when you insert it into the turnstiles that allow you access to the tracks. When you pull it out, the turnstile will open and you may pass. *Be sure to save this ticket throughout your journey!*

- If you purchased a ScotRail Smart Card pass, just hold it up to the validation machine on the platform when you start *and* end your journey.

- Most trains departing Edinburgh to cities within Scotland do not need to be pre-booked. Just buy your ticket at Waverley Station.

Edinburgh Waverley Rail Station website:

www.networkrail.co.uk/communities/passengers/our-stations/edinburgh-waverley

Tramway Clues

If you'll be in Edinburgh for a long stay, take the time to learn the Trams system. It can get you around town quickly and with no traffic jams to hold you up. The fare for the Tram is around £2

There's a Tram line linking Edinburgh and the EDI Airport but we think the Airlink Bus 100 is more convenient. If you want to take the tram you can catch it in the city center along Princes Street. The tramway offers mobile ticketing through their website at:

http://edinburghtrams.com/tickets/mobile-ticketing

PART 10
[Important Final Clues]

Free Sights
Main Museums
Performance Spaces
Festivals & Events
Nightlife
Tipping
& Safety

There are Outlander film locations all over Scotland, like Jamie's Edinburgh print shop

©Alán Duke

Free Sights & Museums:

Arthur's Seat and Holyrood Park

Calton Hill monuments

Dean Village & the Water of Leith

Greyfriars Kirkyard

Museum of Edinburgh

Museum on the Mound (museum of money)

National Museum of Scotland

Outlander film location (Jamie's print shop)

Princes Street Gardens and the Ross Fountain

Royal Botanic Garden (grounds, but not the glasshouses)

Royal Mile

Scott Monument (free to visit but not to climb)

Scottish National Art Gallery

Scottish National Galleries of Modern Art

Scottish National Portrait Gallery

St. Giles' Cathedral

Victoria Street & Grassmarket Square

Pay to enter - Museums of note:

Camera Obscura (interactive museum attraction)

City Art Centre (changing exhibits)

Museum of Childhood

Royal Scottish Academy (a premier exhibition venue)

Surgeons' Hall Museums (grotesque human artifacts)

The Collective - on Calton Hill

Writer's Museum

Main Performance Spaces:

Artspace

Bedlam Theatre

Church Hill Theatre

Dance Base

Edinburgh Castle Esplanade (seasonal)

Edinburgh Playhouse

Festival Theatre

King's Theatre

Leith Theatre

Queen's Hall

Royal Lyceum Theatre

Summerhall

The Hub (seasonal)

Traverse Theatre

Tynecastle Park Stadium (seasonal)

Usher Hall (home of the Royal Scottish Natl. Orchestra)

Festivals and Events
(in sequential order)

This seemingly exhaustive list barely scratches the surface of things that go on here throughout the year. No matter when you visit, you're bound to run into something festive.

New Year's Observation
January 1st and 2nd
This is the official rest period after all the fun. It lasts for two days during which some museums, restaurants, and shops may be closed.
All banks are closed on January 1st.

Burns' Night
January 25
Poetry readings, lots of haggis, and of course whisky mark this night in honor of the
Scottish poet James Burns

Saint Valentine's Day
February 14th
There are plenty of romantic ways to spend Valentines Day in Edinburgh. Local folk picnic and share a kiss on Calton Hill, or take a sunset stroll along the Water of Leith. Afternoon Tea at the elegant Rhubarb restaurant should also be considered.

Holy Week and Easter
Springtime
Easter is not observed here with bunny decorations and the like, but it is a holiday where Edinburghers spend quality time with their families. There's an Easter service held in the morning at St. Giles' Cathedral.

International Science Festival
Month of April
Visual displays and fascinating scientific demonstrations take place at top venues around the city. Whet your curiosity at one of the fun events.

Beltane Fire Festival
April 30th - from sundown to 1am
The event is held on or near Calton Hill, rain or shine. First there's a pagan procession of creatures and then a stage performance with fire, drums, and acrobatics. Tickets can be purchased through the Beltane Fire Society

May Day
May 1st
This is a major holiday in the UK and Europe, and Edinburgh is no exception. It's their Labor Day. Some museums and stores will be closed, as well as all of the banks.

Early May Bank Holiday
A Monday in early May
Official public holiday where all banks will be closed.

Festival of Museums
Late May
A three-day celebration where Scottish museums offer special nighttime events.

International Children's Festival
Late May
Children are celebrated for a week with entertainments ranging from performance art to interactive theatre.

Edinburgh Marathon
Late May
Runners from the world over take to the streets in this highly competitive race through the city and surrounding area.

Spring Bank Holiday
Monday in Late May
Official public holiday where all banks will be closed.

Edinburgh International Film Festival
Mid to late-June
New movies, and viewings of classic ones, highlight this fun event which draws film lovers from all over the world.

Gay Pride Edinburgh
Weekend in mid-June
Edinburgh shows its gay pride all over the city in June.
Festivities include parties, concerts,
and a big pride parade.

Royal Highland Show
Mid to late-June
All things Scottish celebrated with a county-fair
type of atmosphere.

Royal Week
Traditionally held at the end of June
Queen Elizabeth II used to reside at the Palace of
Holyroodhouse annually while performing a range of
official duties around Scotland. She was always given a
formal welcome by the Lord Mayor in the palace
forecourt, and later she would host a garden party for
some 8,000 Scottish guests.
The Palace of Holyroodhouse used to be closed for the
entire week, but King Charles III has recently shortened
this event.

Edinburgh Jazz & Blues Festival
Mid-July
If you're a jazz aficionado, don't miss this gathering of
musicians from around the world as they showcase
their special style of music.

Early August Bank Holiday
A Monday in early August
Official public holiday where all banks will be closed.

The Edinburgh International Festival
Held from August 1 to 24, 2025
The granddaddy of all festivals, this gathering of
famous world class actors, dancers, musicians, and
orchestras is the most popular event of the year next to
Hogmanay. Tens of thousands of participants and
visitors descend on Edinburgh to enjoy the
performances held in venues all over the city.

The Fringe Festival
Held over three weeks in August
In concurrence with the International Festival, the
Fringe is Edinburgh's beloved gathering of comedians,
eclectic music, and various off-beat performers. Groups
large and small perform in any nook
and cranny they can find.

Edinburgh Military Tattoo
Held over three weeks in August
When the military bands wanted to be part of the
famous Edinburgh International Festival, they started
small, with a performance or two at the bandstand in
the Princes Street Gardens. It has now become a
worldwide massing of military bands, piping, and
choreography with nightly performances on the
glorious esplanade of Castle Rock. Don't miss it. ~
Tickets usually go on sale online in January.

Edinburgh International Book Festival
Held over three weeks in August
The world's largest celebration of the written word is
held at the same time as the International Festival,
when a thousand writers and thinkers from across the
globe come together to read, speak, and perform.

Braemar Gathering of the Highland Games
First Saturday in September
Highland Games have been held in Scotland since the 11th century. The Royal family has been associated with them since the reign of Queen Victoria. Events are held in the village of Braemar.

Autumn Public Holiday
Monday in mid-September
Official public holiday when all government services will be closed.

Michaelmas
September 29th
St. Michael is the patron saint of the sea and sailors and his saint's day is observed annually, especially on the western coastline of Scotland.

Scottish International Storytelling Festival
Mid to late-October
For adults and children alike, this event features venues hosting live storytelling, the sharing of traditions, and many different cultural exchanges.

Halloween - October 31st
As the last day of the year in the old Celtic calendar, it was celebrated by the Druids as *Samhuinn* which means "summer ending." It was long associated with witches, bonfires, and costumed children carrying *neep lanterns* (turnips with a candle inside.)
Modern festivities include ghost tours, haunted nights at certain castles, and the city's own vivid display of fire, drumming, and acrobatics courtesy of the Beltane Fire Society. Tickets required for all.

Guy Fawkes Bonfire Night
November 5th
Guy Fawkes tried to blow up London's Houses of
Parliament with twenty barrels of gunpowder in 1605.
Bonfires and fireworks in Edinburgh (and beyond)
help to celebrate his capture.

St. Andrew's Day
November 30th
The day of Scotland's patron saint means the city
observes an official bank holiday.

Edinburgh's Winter Festival
Month of December
Twinkling lights, Christmas Markets, temporary ice
rinks, and Santa turn this town into something
unforgettable. Kids love the seasonal set up in Princes
Street Gardens which features rides and a toy market.
Try to find the Elves' Workshop hidden within a
Christmas tree maze, or visit Santa's Grotto
to meet the elf himself.

Sowans Nicht / Christmas Eve
December 24th
The Christmas observance begins citywide. This is the
final day of the Christmas Markets.

Christmas Day
December 25th
Many museums, restaurants, pubs, and shops, as well
as all banks, will be closed.

Boxing Day
December 26th

The Christmas holiday continues on this day, when boxed gifts used to be exchanged. Many museums, restaurants, pubs, and shops, as well as all banks, will be closed.

Hogmanay
The Scottish New Year's celebration
December 30th through January 2nd

Hogmanay is more important here than Christmas. There's a huge (ticketed) street party on Prince Street but you can just as easily pick any pub in which to celebrate. The bells of the city chime midnight and *Auld Lang Syne* is sung by all. The official rest period after all the fun will last through January 2nd. Note that some museums, shops, restaurants, and banks will be closed.

The nightlife here is more than just pubs

©Alán Duke

Nightlife in Edinburgh

Edinburgh has a lot going on at night, from theatre and traditional live music to pumping nightclubs and chic cocktail lounges. And then there are the eighty-or-so pubs to figure in. Let's just say there's definitely something for everyone. The main cluster of gay bars can be found in an eastern section of town near the corner of Leith Walk and Blenheim Place.

The city's hottest spots are ever-changing. For the most current recommendations and performances, tap your hotel concierge. They will know just what to recommend. In the meantime, here's our personal short list:

Cocktails & mixology

Panda & Sons
Speakeasy that can be mistaken for a barber shop
Head downstairs and proceed through the bookcase,
if you can figure out how to open it.
Unique, tasty mixology
Located at 79 Queen Street, in the New Town

Bramble
Top-rated cocktail bar appreciated by those in the know
Order one of their namesake house cocktails
Located in the basement of 16 Queen Street, in the New Town
Request way ahead by email for a table:
tables@bramblebar.co.uk

Well-established club scenes:

Sneaky Pete's
Busy, sweaty grunge club under the George IV Bridge
Located at 75 Cowgate in the Old Town
Local mobile calling: 0-131-225-1757

The Liquid Room
Huge venue housed in a former church,
enter through the door on the front right.
Located at 9 Victoria Street in the Old Town
Local mobile calling: 0-131-225-2564

The Voodoo Rooms
Opulent bar and ballroom,
with live events and great cocktails.
Located at 19a West Register Street in the New Town
Local mobile calling: 0-131-556-7060

Live folk music hotspots:

Sandy Bell's
World-famous folk music bar
Located at 25 Forrest Road in the Old Town
Local mobile calling: 0-131-225-2751

Whiski Bar
Pretty pub with live music every night
Located at 109 High Street (Royal Mile) Old Town
Local mobile calling: 0-131-556-3095

The Doric Tavern
17th century gastropub near Waverley Station
Live music on Fridays & Saturdays
Located at 36 Blair Street in the city center
Local mobile calling: 0-131-225-1084

Captain's Bar
Live acoustical music in a real Scottish pub
Should be reopening soon
4 South College Street in the Old Town
Local mobile calling: 0-749-355-5702

Tipping Clues

Unlike some guide books, tourist websites, and articles touting so-called travel advice, we're going to be completely honest here and go against all that "useful" information about tipping in Edinburgh.

In restaurants, never ask if the tip or service is included because you won't necessarily get a straight answer. The servers are paid a fair, living wage and there is some service fee built into the check, along with the tax. All you have to do is pay the total and leave.

If you really want to show that you appreciated the service, leave an extra 10% in cash. Note that in hotels the tip for housekeeping is already included in your room fees. Here are some other specifics:

Taxis: Round up to the nearest British Pound

Shuttle Bus driver: Zero tip

Hotel concierge: £5 to £20 if they got you tickets that were impossible to find.

Hotel room housekeeper: Zero tip

Bellman: £2 to £5 if they bring your baggage to the room.

Bathroom attendants: £1, unless there's a sign stating an expected amount.

Coat checks: Zero tip

Hair stylist: Zero tip

Tour guides: Tip at your discretion if you enjoyed their banter.

Cafés and bars: Zero tip

Money Clues

American debit cards work fine at Scotland's ATMs but be careful about trying to take out too much cash at once or on the same day. Find out what your daily withdrawal limit is *in British Pounds* so that you don't wonder why your bank card has been rejected in Edinburgh.

For the best exchange rate, get your cash out of an ATM that is located at or owned by an actual bank, such as *Barclays*, *HSBC* or the *Bank of Scotland,* rather than one that is operated by a private money "exchange" company; their ATM machines look just like the bank's in order to deceive you, so go by the name that's advertised on them.

Use your bank's debit card for purchases wisely. Since there may be a fee with each use, you might not want to debit that £3 beer. The fee will be more than the drink! Try to find a travel-friendly, fee-free debit credit card like Capital One before your trip.

Some banks and credit card companies still appreciate a phone call to let them know you'll be traveling abroad. Call them just in case to avoid any hassles in the UK.

Spend all of your UK coins by the end of your visit because they're not exchangeable at all.

In Edinburgh, hotels and rental properties may charge a small tourist room tax per person, per night in cash. Just be ready for it or ask about it in advance.

Visitors are no longer eligible for VAT tax refunds in the UK. The government found it too expensive to sustain, but there is talk that this was a huge mistake for their economy and that it might be put back in place next year.

Telephone Clues

Telephone numbers in Edinburgh are usually seven digits long. The country code for the United Kingdom is 44 and the area code for Edinburgh is 131.

Calling Edinburgh from the U.S. or Canada:

Dial 011, then 44 (UK), then 131 (Edinburgh), and then the phone number.
If the phone number is 465-8812, you would dial: 011-44-131-465-8812.

Calling the U.S. or Canada from Edinburgh:

Dial 001, then the U.S. area code or Canadian city code, plus the basic phone number.
You might first hear a recording verifying that you're about to make an international call; just stay on the line as this is perfectly normal.

Calling from within Edinburgh, to Edinburgh

From a landline - Dial the seven digits of the basic phone number. That's it!

From a cell phone - Dial starting with 0-131 (Edinburgh) and then the basic phone number.

Your Consulate

If for any reason you feel you need to reach out to your Consulate General, (passport problems, safety, legal problems, etc.) here is the necessary information:

American Consulate in Edinburgh:
Local mobile calling: 0-131-556-8315
International calling: (011) 44-131-556-8315
-Located at 3 Regent Terrace, Edinburgh, Scotland

Canadian Consulate servicing Edinburgh:
-Local mobile calling: 44-7702-359-916

British Consulate in Edinburgh:
Local mobile calling: 0-131-524-5700
International calling: (0044) 131-524-5700
-Located at 2/4 Waterloo Place, Edinburgh, Scotland

Edinburgh has some amazing ruins,
like these at Craigmillar Castle

©Alán Duke

Safety and Common Sense

Edinburgh, for all its millions of visitors, is a very safe city but that doesn't mean you should let down your guard. A bit of caution and common sense can go a long way so protect your valuables the same way you would anywhere, by using the electronic safe in your hotel room and by keeping money tucked away out of sight. Be wary of pick-pockets, especially if you find yourself in a crowded area like Edinburgh Castle.

Bathrooms are available to all who need them at nearly every sight, museum, and café. Just inquire politely and you'll be directed to it without hesitation.

Feeling ill? There are pharmacies all over Edinburgh. Look for storefronts indicated with the symbol of a cross. Your hotel can call a medical professional for you if required— another good reason to stay at a full-service hotel rather than in a private apartment.

The tap water in Edinburgh is safe for most travelers to drink and you can ask your waiter for a glass or carafe of it for free.

Scotland has a different electrical current than the U.S., and to make matters more difficult, the plug style (and shape) that allows you to connect to an electrical outlet is even different between Scotland and Paris. This means you need to be prepared. Take a couple of plug adaptors with you, the more the better. Don't worry, they're cheap and can be ordered on amazon.com which is much easier than running all over town trying to find them. Plan in advance!

We don't recommend taking *electrical converters* with you because we don't trust them. They rarely work on things like blow dryers, even though the companies making them claim that they will convert the electrical current on any appliance. Most decent hotels supply a blow dryer for you because it's cheaper than paying to repair that burned room.

As for your iPhone, laptop, or other high-tech toy...they're already made dual-voltage so the only thing you need to worry about is getting that plug adapter so you can actually plug it into the wall socket!

Emergency? Dial 999

From the Authors

We've had so much fun bringing this book to you and sincerely hope you found it useful. The star rating offered to you at the end is for metadata use only and does not affect our online stars. If you enjoyed *Clued In Edinburgh*, please take a moment to leave a short customer review on Amazon.com so that your rating will count for us. Even a few sentences would be greatly appreciated.

Our blog is easily accessible and offers additional information to travelers between our annual updates. We also field any and all questions, comments, advice, and suggestions at cluedintravelbooks@gmail.com.

If you're looking for experiences that will take your Scottish visit to the next level, check out our super fun *Bored in Edinburgh -Awesome Experiences for the Repeat Visitor*, now at Amazon.com:

www.amazon.com/dp/B0CTGJWV7S

Thank you so much for your support. Check out our other cool *Clued In* travel books:

Clued In London

Clued In Venice

Clued In Paris

Clued In Rome

Clued In Florence

Clued In Barcelona

Clued In Munich

Clued In New York

Clued In Miami

For more information on this or other
© Clued In travel books,
visit our city-by-city blog at
www.cluedintravelbooks.com

Disclaimer

Every effort has been made for accuracy. All weblinks and URL's herein were accurate and live at the time of publishing, but travel information is fluid and prone to change. The authors, publishers, and webmasters take no responsibility for consequences or mishaps while using this book, nor are they responsible for any difficulties, inconveniences, injuries, illness, medical conditions, or other physical issues related to the information and suggestions provided in this book. The information contained in this book is for diversionary purposes only. In addition, no mentions in this book represent or indicate an endorsement of any site, group or company or their practices, methods, or accidents that may occur when visited, hired, joined, or participated in.

In no event will we be liable for any loss or damage direct or indirect or any loss or damage whatsoever arising from a loss of profits or the like arising out of, or in connection with, the use of this eBook or print book.

In this eBook or print book, the links provided are not under the control of *Clued In Travel Books* or its authors or associates and they have no control over the nature, content, or the availability of those websites. Furthermore, the inclusion of any links does not imply a recommendation or endorsement of reflect the views of the authors of *Clued In Travel Books*. Every effort has been made to provide live links that are up to date and working properly but this cannot be guaranteed in all instances.

My notes

My notes

Made in United States
Orlando, FL
09 April 2025

60337873R00128